Among the Isles of Shoals

WHITE ISLAND, LOOKING SOUTHWEST FROM APPLEDORE.

Celia Thaxter, circa 1875
Courtesy University of New Hampshire

Among the
ISLES OF SHOALS

Celia Thaxter

University Press of New England
Hanover and London

Published by University Press of New England,
One Court Street, Lebanon, NH 03766
www.upne.com

First University Press of New England edition 2003

Printed in the United States of America
5 4 3 2

ISBN–13: 978–1–58465–330–1
ISBN–10: 1–58465–330–2

This facsimile edition includes additional photographs from the collections of the University of New Hampshire, the Portsmouth Public Library, Joseph P. Copley, and Peter E. Randall.

The Library of Congress has cataloged the original edition as follows:
Thaxter, Celia Laighton, 1835–1894.
  Among the Isles of Shoals / by Celia Thaxter
    p.   cm.
  Originally published: Boston : J. R. Osgood, 1873
  Includes index.
  ISBN 0–914339–49–4
  1. Isles of Shoals (Me. and N.H.) — Description and travel.
2. Isles of Shoals (Me. and N.H.) — History. 3. Thaxter, Celia
Laighton, 1835–1894. I. Title.
  F42.I8T3   1994
  974.1'95 — dc20   94–17969

Among the Isles of Shoals.

By CELIA THAXTER.

𝔚ith 𝔍llustrations.

"Only to hear and see the far-off sparkling brine."
TENNYSON.

BOSTON
HOUGHTON, MIFFLIN AND COMPANY
New York : 85 Fifth Avenue
𝔗he 𝔯iverside 𝔭ress, 𝔠ambridge

LIST OF ILLUSTRATIONS.

———◆———

IT is with reluctance that I suffer these fragmentary and inadequate sketches of the Isles of Shoals to appear in book form. Except that some account of the place, however slight, is so incessantly called for by people who throng these islands in summer, I should hardly venture to offer to the public so imperfect a chronicle, of which the most that can be said is, that it is, perhaps, better than nothing.

AMONG THE ISLES OF SHOALS.

N a series of papers published not many years ago, Herman Melville made the world acquainted with the "Encantadas," or Enchanted Islands, which he describes as lying directly under the equator, off the coast of South America, and of which he says: "It is to be doubted whether any spot of earth can, in desolateness, furnish a parallel to this group." But their dark volcanic crags and melancholy beaches can hardly seem more desolate than do the low bleached rocks of the Isles of Shoals to eyes that behold them for the first time. Very sad they look, stern, bleak, and unpromising, yet are they enchanted islands in a better sense of the word than are the great Gallipagos of which Mr. Melville discourses so delightfully.

There is a strange charm about them, an indescribable influence in their atmosphere, hardly to be explained, but universally acknowledged. People forget the hurry and worry and fret of life after living there awhile, and, to an imaginative mind, all things become dreamy as they were to the lotus-eaters, to whom

> " The gushing of the wave
> Far, far away did seem to mourn and rave
> On alien shores."

The eternal sound of the sea on every side has a tendency to wear away the edge of human thought and perception; sharp outlines become blurred and softened like a sketch in charcoal; nothing appeals to the mind with the same distinctness as on the mainland, amid the rush and stir of people and things, and the excitements of social life. This was strikingly illustrated during the late war, which, while it wrung the heart of the whole country, and stirred the blood of every man, woman, and child on the continent, left the handful of human beings upon these lonely rocks almost untouched. The echoes of woe and terror were so faint and far they seemed to lose their significance among the many-voiced waters they crossed, and reached at last the indifferent ears they sought with no more force than a spent wave.

Nine miles of the Atlantic Ocean intervene between these islands and the nearest point of the coast of New Hampshire; but from this nearest point the coast-line recedes gradually, in dim and dimmer distance, to Cape Ann, in Massachusetts, twenty-one miles away at the southwest, and to Cape Neddock, in Maine, sixteen miles distant in the northeast (in clear weather another cape is faintly distinguishable beyond this), and about one third of the great horizon is filled by this beautiful, undulating line of land, which, under the touch of atmospheric change, is almost as plastic as the clouds, and wears a new aspect with every turn of wind and weather.

Sailing out from Portsmouth Harbor with a fair wind from the northwest, the Isles of Shoals lie straight before you, nine miles away, — ill-defined and cloudy shapes, faintly discernible in the distance. A word about the origin of this name, "Isles of Shoals." They are supposed to have been so called, not because the ragged reefs run out beneath the water in all directions, ready to wreck and destroy, but because of the "shoaling," or "schooling," of fish about them, which, in the mackerel and herring seasons, is remarkable. As you approach they separate, and show each its own peculiar characteristics, and you perceive that there are six islands if the tide is low; but if it is

1 *

high, there are eight, and would be nine, but that a breakwater connects two of them.   Appledore, called for many years Hog Island, from its rude resemblance to a hog's back rising from the water, when seen from out at sea, is the largest and most regular in shape.   From afar, it looks smoothly rounded, like a gradually sloping elevation, the greatest height of which is only seventy-five feet above high-water mark.   A little valley in which are situated the buildings belonging to the house of entertainment, which is the only habitation, divides its four hundred acres into two unequal portions.   Next, almost within a stone's throw, is Haley's Island, or "Smutty-nose," so christened by passing sailors, with a grim sense of humor, from a long black point of rock stretching out to the southeast, upon which many a ship has laid her bones.   This island is low and flat, and contains a greater depth of soil than the others.   At low tide, Cedar and Malaga are both connected with it, — the latter permanently by a breakwater, — the whole comprising about one hundred acres. Star Island contains one hundred and fifty acres, and lies a quarter of a mile southwest of Smutty-nose.   Toward its northern end are clustered the houses of the little village of Gosport, with a tiny church crowning the highest rock.   Not quite a mile southwest from Star, White Island lifts a lighthouse for a warning. This is the most picturesque of the group, and forms, with Seavey's Island, at low water, a double island, with an area of some twenty acres. Most westerly lies Londoner's, an irregular rock with a bit of beach, upon which all the shells about the cluster seem to be thrown. Two miles northeast from Appledore, Duck Island thrusts out its lurking ledges on all sides beneath the water, one of them running half a mile to the northwest. This is the most dangerous of the islands, and, being the most remote, is the only one visited to any great degree by the shy sea-fowl that are nearly banished by civilization. Yet even now, at low tide, those long black ledges are often whitened by the dazzling plumage of gulls whose exquisite and stainless purity rivals the new-fallen snow. The ledges run toward the west and north; but at the east and south the shore is bolder, and Shag and Mingo Rocks, where, during or after storms, the sea breaks with magnificent effect, lie isolated by a narrow channel from the main granite fragment. A very round rock west of Londoner's, perversely called "Square," and Anderson's Rock, off the southeast end of Smutty-nose, complete the catalogue.

Smutty-nose and Appledore are almost united

by a reef, bare at low tide, though a large vessel can pass between them even then. Off the landing at White Island the Devil's Rock rolls an incessant breaker, and makes an attempt to reach the shore perilous in any but the serenest weather. Between Londoner's and Star is another, hardly bare at low tide; a perpetual danger, for it lies directly in the path of most of the sailing vessels, and many a schooner has been "brought up all standing" by this unexpected obstacle. Another rock, about four miles east of Appledore, rejoices in the significant title of the "Old Harry." Old Harry is deeply sunk beneath the surface, and never betrays himself except in great storms, when an awful white spray rises afar off, and the Shoalers know how tremendous are the breakers that send it skyward.

The names of the towns, Appledore, Gosport, and, along the coast, Portsmouth, Newcastle, Rye, Ipswich, Portland, Bangor, Newbury, Amesbury, Salisbury, and many more, are all borrowed from towns on, or not far from, the coasts of England and Wales, as may be seen from the maps of those countries. Salisbury Beach fronts our islands. Amesbury lies farther inland, but the gentle outline of Po Hill, in that town, is the last eminence of any importance on the southern end of the coast line.

The dividing line between Maine and New Hampshire passes through the group, giving Appledore, Smutty-nose, and Duck Islands to Maine, and the rest to New Hampshire; but their allegiance to either is a matter of small importance, the few inhabitants troubling themselves but little about what State they belong to. Till within a few years no taxes were required of them, and they enjoyed immunity from this and various other earthly ills as completely as the gulls and loons that shared their dwelling-place.

Swept by every wind that blows, and beaten by the bitter brine for unknown ages, well may the Isles of Shoals be barren, bleak, and bare. At first sight nothing can be more rough and inhospitable than they appear. The incessant influences of wind and sun, rain, snow, frost, and spray, have so bleached the tops of the rocks, that they look hoary as if with age, though in the summer-time a gracious greenness of vegetation breaks here and there the stern outlines, and softens somewhat their rugged aspect. Yet so forbidding are their shores, it seems scarcely worth while to land upon them,— mere heaps of tumbling granite in the wide and lonely sea,— when all the smiling, "sapphire-spangled marriage-ring of the land" lies ready to woo the voyager back again, and welcome

his returning prow with pleasant sights and sounds
and scents that the wild wastes of water never
know.   But to the human creature who has eyes
that will see and ears that will hear, nature appeals with such a novel charm, that the luxurious
beauty of the land is half forgotten before one is
aware.   Its sweet gardens, full of color and perfume, its rich woods and softly swelling hills, its
placid waters, and fields and flowery meadows, are
no longer dear and desirable; for the wonderful
sound of the sea dulls the memory of all past im-
pressions, and seems to fulfil and satisfy all present
needs.   Landing for the first time, the stranger is
struck only by the sadness of the place,— the vast
loneliness; for there are not even trees to whisper
with familiar voices, — nothing but sky and sea
and rocks.   But the very wildness and desolation
reveal a strange beauty to him.   Let him wait till
evening comes,

"With sunset purple soothing all the waste,"

and he will find himself slowly succumbing to the
subtile charm of that sea atmosphere.   He sleeps
with all the waves of the Atlantic murmuring in
his ears, and wakes to the freshness of a summer
morning; and it seems as if morning were made for
the first time.   For the world is like a new-blown

rose, and in the heart of it he stands, with only
the caressing music of the water to break the utter
silence, unless, perhaps, a song-sparrow pours out
its blissful warble like an embodied joy. The sea
is rosy, and the sky; the line of land is radiant;
the scattered sails glow with the delicious color
that touches so tenderly the bare, bleak rocks.
These are lovelier than sky or sea or distant sails,
or graceful gulls' wings reddened with the dawn;
nothing takes color so beautifully as the bleached
granite; the shadows are delicate, and the fine,
hard outlines are glorified and softened beneath
the fresh first blush of sunrise. All things are
speckless and spotless; there is no dust, no noise,
nothing but peace in the sweet air and on the
quiet sea. The day goes on; the rose changes to
mellow gold, the gold to clear, white daylight, and
the sea is sparkling again. A breeze ripples the
surface, and wherever it touches the color deepens.
A seine-boat passes, with the tawny net heaped in
the stern, and the scarlet shirts of the rowers brilliant against the blue. Pleasantly their voices
come across the water, breaking the stillness. The
fishing-boats steal to and fro, silent, with glittering
sails; the gulls wheel lazily; the far-off coasters
glide rapidly along the horizon; the mirage steals
down the coast-line, and seems to remove it leagues

away. And what if it were to slip down the slope of the world and disappear entirely? You think, in a half-dream, you would not care. Many troubles, cares, perplexities, vexations, lurk behind that far, faint line for you. Why should you be bothered any more?

> " Let us alone. Time driveth onward fast,
> And in a little while our lips are dumb."

And so the waves, with their lulling murmur, do their work, and you are soothed into repose and transient forgetfulness.

The natives, or persons who have been brought up here, find it almost as difficult to tear themselves away from the islands as do the Swiss to leave their mountains. From a civilized race's point of view, this is a curious instance of human perversity, since it is not good for men to live their whole lives through in such remote and solitary places. Nobody hears of people dying of homesickness for New York, or Albany, or Maine, or California, or any place on the broad continent; but to wild and lonely spots like these isles humanity clings with an intense and abiding affection. No other place is able to furnish the inhabitants of the Shoals with sufficient air for their capacious lungs; there is never scope enough elsewhere, there is no horizon; they must have sea-room. On shore it is to them as if all the trees and houses crowded against the windows to suffocation; and I know a youth who, when at the age of thirteen he made his first visit to the mainland, descended to the cellar of the house in which he found himself, in the not over-populous city of Portsmouth, and spent the few hours of his stay sitting dejectedly upon a wood-pile, in mute protest against the condition of things in general, and the pressure of human society in particular.

Each island has its peculiar characteristics, as I said before, and no two are alike, though all are of the same coarse granite, mixed with masses and seams of quartz and felspar and gneiss and mica-slate, and interspersed with dikes of trap running in all directions. Upon Appledore, for the most part, the trap runs from north to south, while the veins of quartz and felspar run from east to west. Sometimes the narrow white quartz veins intersect the dark trap, in parallel lines, now wavering, and now perfectly straight, and showing a surface like that of some vast piece of inlaid work. Each island presents its boldest shore to the east, to breast the whole force of the great Atlantic, which every year assails the iron cliffs and headlands with the same ponderous fury, yet leaves

upon them so little trace of its immense power, —
though at White Island, on the top of a precipi-
tous rock called "The Head," which is nearly fifty
feet high, lies a bowlder weighing fifteen tons,
tossed there from below by the breakers. The
shores are seldom very bold, but on the east they
are often very striking with their rifts and chasms,
and roughly piled gorges, and square quarries of
stone, and stairways cut as if by human hands.
The trap rock, softer than the granite, is worn
away in many places, leaving bare perpendicular
walls fifteen or twenty feet high. The largest trap
dike upon Appledore runs across the island from
northeast to southwest, disappears in the sea, and
reappears upon Smutty-nose, a quarter of a mile
distant in a straight line. In some places, the ge-
ologist will tell you, certain deep scratches in the
solid rock mean that here the glacier ground its
way across in the world's earlier ages. Frequently
the trap rock is honeycombed in a curious fashion,
— filled with small holes on the surface, as if drops
of water falling for years in the same spots had
worn these smooth round hollows. This always
happens close to the water, and only in the trap
rock, and looks as if it might be the result of the
flying spray which, in winter and toward spring,
when the northwest gales blow sometimes for three

TRAP DIKE, APPLEDORE.

The Oceanic Hotel on Star island was completed in 1873, the year this book was printed. It was destroyed by fire two years later.

Guests on the porch of the first Oceanic Hotel on Star island.

weeks steadily day and night, beats continually upon the shore.

The coast-line varies, of course, with high or low tide. At low water the shores are much more forbidding than at high tide, for a broad band of dark sea-weed girdles each island, and gives a sullen aspect to the whole group. But in calm days, when the moon is full and the tides are so low that it sometimes seems as if the sea were being drained away on purpose to show to eager eyes what lies beneath the lowest ebb, banks of golden-green and brown moss thickly clustered on the moist ledges are exposed, and the water is cut by the ruffled edges of the kelps that grow in brown and shining forests on every side. At sunrise or sunset the effect of the long rays slanting across these masses of rich color is very beautiful. But at high tide the shores are most charming; every little cove and inlet is filled with the music of the waves, and their life, light, color, and sparkle. Who shall describe that wonderful noise of the sea among the rocks, to me the most suggestive of all the sounds in nature? Each island, every isolated rock, has its own peculiar rote, and ears made delicate by listening, in great and frequent peril, can distinguish the bearings of each in a dense fog. The threatening speech of Duck

Island's ledges, the swing of the wave over Half-way Rock, the touch of the ripples on the beach at Londoner's, the long and lazy breaker that is forever rolling below the lighthouse at White Island, — all are familiar and distinct, and indicate to the islander his whereabouts almost as clearly as if the sun shone brightly and no shrouding mist were striving to mock and to mislead him.

There are no beaches of any considerable size along the circle of these shores, and except in two narrow fissures, one on Malaga and one on Star, only a few feet wide at their widest, there is no fine, clean sand, such as lies sparkling on the coast at Rye, opposite, and shows, faintly glimmering, white in the far distance. The dock at Smutty-nose is filled with coarse sand and mud, like the little basin of the "Upper Cove" on Appledore; and the largest beach on Star, of the same character, is covered with a stratum of fish-bones several feet deep, — by no means a pleasantly fragrant pavement. Roughly rounded pebbles, not beautiful with warmth of color like those on the Cohasset beaches, but a cold, hard combination of gray granite and dark trap, are heaped in the coves. Indian arrowheads of jasper and flint have been found among them. Now and then a smoother bit consists of a coarse gravel, which, if you ex-

amine, you will find to be principally composed of
shells ground fine by the waves, a fascinating mixture of blue and purple mussels, lined with the
rainbow tints of mother-of-pearl, and fragments of
golden and ruddy snail-shells, and striped and colored cockles ; with here and there a piece of transparent quartz, white or rosy, or of opaque felspar,
faintly straw-colored, or of dull-purple porphyry
stone, all clean and moist with the odorous brine.
Upon Appledore and the little islets undevastated
by civilization these tiny coves are the most delightful places in the world, lovely with their fringe
of weeds, thistles, and mullein-stalks drawn clearly
against the sky at the upper edge of the slope,
and below, their mosaic of stone and shell and
sea-wrack, tangles of kelp and driftwood, — a mass
of warm neutral tints, — with brown, green, and
crimson mosses, and a few golden snail-shells lying
on the many-tinted gravel, where the indolent
ripples lapse in delicious murmurs. There are few
shells more delicate than the variegated snails and
cockles and stout whelks that sparsely strew the
beaches, but these few are exceedingly beautiful,
and more precious from their rarity. Two kinds
of pure white spiral shells, not quite an inch long,
are occasionally found, and cause one to wonder
how they can be rolled together with the heavy
pebbles by the breakers and not be annihilated.

After the dark blue mussel-shells have lain long on shore in sun and rain, they take a curious satin sheen, lovely to behold, and the larger kind, shedding their coat of brown varnish, are colored like the eastern sky in clear winter sunsets, a rosy purple, with pearly linings streaked with iridescent hues. The driftwood is always full of suggestions : — a broken oar ; a bit of spar with a ragged end of rope-yarn attached ; a section of a mast hurriedly chopped, telling of a tragedy too well known on the awful sea ; a water-worn buoy, or flakes of rich brown bark, which have been peacefully floated down the rivers of Maine and out on the wide sea, to land at last here and gladden firesides so remote from the deep green wood where they grew ; pine-cones, with their spicy fragrance yet lingering about them ; apples, green spruce twigs, a shingle, with some carpenter's half-obliterated calculations pencilled upon it ; a child's roughly carved boat ; drowned butterflies, beetles, birds ; dead boughs of ragged fir-trees completely draped with the long, shining ribbon-grass that grows in brackish water near river mouths. The last, after lying awhile in the wind and sun, present a weird appearance, for the narrow ribbons are dried and bleached as white as chalk, and shiver and shudder with every wind that blows. It used to be a great delight to hold such a bough aloft, and watch all the long, delicate pennons and streamers fly trembling out on the breeze. Beyond high-water mark all things in the course of time take a uniform gray color from the weather; wood, shells, stones, deposited by some great tide or storm, and left undisturbed for months, chocolate-colored bark and yellow shingle and gray stone are not to be distinguished one from another, except by their shape. Of course all white things grow whiter, and shells already colorless become as pure as snow. Sometimes the slabs and blocks of wood that float ashore have drifted so long that they are water-logged, and covered with a rich growth of mosses, barnacles, and wondrous sea-creatures. Sometimes they are completely riddled by the pholas, and the hardest shells are pierced smoothly through and through by these soft worms.

But as a child I was never without apprehension when examining the drift, for I feared to find some too dreadful token of disaster. After the steamer Bohemian was wrecked (off Halifax, I think) a few years ago, bales of her costly cargo of silks and rich stuffs and pieces of the wreck were strewn along the coast even to Cape Ann; and upon Rye Beach, among other things, two boots came on shore. They were not mates, and each contained a human foot. That must have been a grewsome discovery to him who picked them up.

There are not many of these quiet coves. In general a confusion reigns as if an earthquake had rent and split the coasts, and tumbled the masses in chaotic heaps. On Appledore and the larger islands the interior is rather smoother, though no-where will you find many rods of plain walking. Slopes of greenness alternate with the long white ledges, and here and there are bits of swampy ground and little valleys where the turf is short, and the sheep love to browse, and the mushrooms grow in August and September. There are no trees except, perhaps, a few balm-of-gilead trees on Star and a small elm on Appledore, which has been struggling with the bleakness of the situation some twenty years. It is very probable that the islands were wooded many years ago with spruce and pine perhaps, — a rugged growth. I am certain that cedars grew there, for I found on the highest part of Smutty-nose Point, deep down in a crevice in the rocks, a piece of a root of cedar-wood, which, though perfectly preserved, bore marks of great age, being worn as smooth as glass with the rain-drops that had penetrated to its hiding-place. There are a few bushes, browsed down by the sheep, with maple, poplar, and birch leaves; and I have seen the crumbling remains of the stump of some large tree in the principal gorge or valley at Appledore. The oldest inhabitants remember quite an orchard on Smutty-nose. In the following note (for which I am indebted to Mr. T. B. Fox) from "Christopher Leavitt's Voyage into New England" in the year 1623, it appears that there were trees, though not of the kind the voyagers wished to see. He says: "The first place I set my foot upon in New England was the Isles of Shoulds. We could see not one good timber tree, or so much good ground as to make a garden. Good fishing-place for six ships," he goes on to say, "not more for want of good storage rooms. Harbor indifferent good. No savages at all." That was two hundred and forty-six years ago. In the Rev. Jedediah Morse's journal of a mission to the Shoals in August, 1800, he says, referring to the wretched state of the inhabitants of Star Island at that time, "All the trees, and the bushes even, have been consumed, and they have cut up, dried, and burned many acres of the sward, leaving only naked rocks where formerly there was the finest pasturage for cows." The bushes have never grown again on Star; but Appledore, wherever there is soil enough to hold a root, is overgrown

2

with huckleberry and bayberry bushes, the glossy green leaves of the latter yielding a wholesome, aromatic fragrance, which accords well with the fresh and healthy sea-odors. Blackberry, raspberry, wild currant, and gooseberry bushes also flourish ; there are clumps of elder and sumach, woodbine and the poison ivy, shrubs of wild-cherry and shadbush, and even one little wild apple-tree that yearly bears a few large, bright blossoms.

It is curious to note the varieties of plants, wild-flowers, and grasses on this island alone. There are six different ferns, and many delicate flowers bloom in the spring, whose faces it is a continual surprise to find looking up at you from the rough ground, among the rocks. Every flower seems twice as beautiful under these circumstances ; and it is a fact that the salt air and a peculiar richness in the soil give a luxuriance of growth and a depth of color not found elsewhere. "Is that willow-weed" (or whatever it may be)? "I never saw any so bright !" is a remark often heard from strangers visiting the islands for the first time. The pale-pink herb-robert, for instance, blushes with a tint almost as deep as a damask rose, and as for the wild-roses, I heard some one say they were as "bright as red carnations." In the spring the anemones are stained with purple and pink

and yellow in a way that makes their sisters of
the mainland seem pallid beside them; and the
violets are wonderful, — the blue ones so large
and dark, and the delicately-veined white ones rich
with creamy fragrance.

The calyx of the shadbush-flower is dyed with
purple, almost crimson, and the color runs into
the milky whiteness of the petals. The little
pimpernel (when it has anything but salt gravel to
grow in, for it runs fairly into the sea) is clear
vermilion, and the pearly eyebright is violet on
the edges; the shy celandine glows golden in its
shady clefts, and the spotted jewel-weed is as rich
and splendid as a flower in Doctor Rappacini's famous garden. Sometimes it is as if the order of
nature were set aside in this spot; for you find the
eyebright and pimpernel and white violets growing side by side until the frost comes in November; often October passes with no sign of frost,
and the autumn lingers later than elsewhere. I
have even seen the iris and wild-rose and golden-rod
and aster in blossom together, as if, not having
the example of the world before their eyes, they
followed their own sweet will, and bloomed when
they took the fancy. As for garden flowers, when
you plant them in this soil they fairly run mad
with color. People say, "Do give me some seeds

of these wonderful flowers"; and they sow them
in their gardens on the mainland, and they come
up decorous, commonplace, and pale, like their sisters in the same soil.   The little spot of earth on
which they grow at the island is like a mass of
jewels.   Who shall describe the pansies, richly
streaked with burning gold; the dark velvet core-
opsis and the nasturtium; the larkspurs, blue and
brilliant as lapis-lazuli; the "ardent marigolds,"
that flame like mimic suns?   The sweet-peas are
of a deep, bright rose-color, and their odor is like
rich wine, too sweet almost to be borne, except
when the pure fragrance of mignonette is added,
— such mignonette as never grows on shore.
Why should the poppies blaze in such imperial
scarlet?   What quality is hidden in this thin soil,
which so transfigures all the familiar flowers with
fresh beauty?   I have heard it said that it is the
crumbled rock which so enriches the earth, but I
do not know.

If a flock of sheep and various cows did not
browse over Appledore incessantly, it would be a
little wilderness of wild-flowers in the summer;
they love the soil and climate, and put forth all
their strength and loveliness.   And every year or
two a new kind appears, of which the seed has
been brought by some bird, or, perhaps, shaken

out of a bundle of hay. Last summer, for the first time, I found the purple polygala growing in a meadowy piece of turf on the south side of the island. Columbines and the fragrant ground-nut, helianthus, and various other plants, grow only on Duck Island; and it is singular that the little potentilla, which I am told grows elsewhere only on mountain-sides, is found here on all the islands. At Smutty-nose alone certain plants of the wicked-looking henbane (*Hyoscyamus niger*) flourish, and, on Londoner's only, there spreads at the top of the beach a large sea-lungwort (*Mertensia maritima*). At Star the crooked little ways between the houses are lined with tall plants of the poisonous hemlock (the *Conium* that made the death-draught of Socrates), which flourishes amain, and is the only green thing out of the small walled enclosures, except the grass and the burdocks; for the cows and the children devastate the ground.

Appledore is altogether the most agreeable in its aspect of all the islands, being the largest, and having a greater variety of surface than the rest. Its southern portion is full of interest, from the traces of vanished humanity which one beholds at every step; for the ground in some places is undermined with ancient graves, and the ruined cellars of houses wherein men and women lived more

than a century ago are scattered here and there
to the number of seventy and more. The men and
women are dust and ashes; but here are the stones
they squared and laid; here are the thresholds
over which so many feet have passed. The pale
green and lilac and golden lichens have overgrown
and effaced all traces of their footsteps on the door-
stones; but here they passed in and out, —old and
young, little feet of children, heavy tramp of stal-
wart fishermen, lighter tread of women, painful and
uncertain steps of age. Pleasant it is to think of
the brown and swarthy fisherman, the father, standing on such a threshold, and with the keen glance
all seafaring men possess sweeping the wide horizon for signs of fair or foul weather; or the
mother, sitting in the sun on the step, nursing
her baby, perhaps, or mending a net, or spinning,
— for the women here were famous spinners, and
on Star Island yet are women who have not forgotten the art. Pleasanter still to think of some
slender girl at twilight lingering with reluctant
feet, and wistful eyes that search the dusky sea for
a returning sail whose glimmer is sweeter than
moonlight or starlight to her sight, — lingering
still, though her mother calls within and the dew
falls with the falling night. I love to people these
solitudes again, and think that those who lived

here centuries ago were decent, God-fearing folk, most of them, — for so tradition says;* though in later years they fell into evil ways, and drank "fire-water," and came to grief. And all the pictures over which I dream are set in this framework of the sea, that sparkled and sang, or frowned and threatened, in the ages that are gone as it does to-day, and will continue to smile and threaten when we who listen to it and love it and fear it now are dust and ashes in our turn.

Some of the cellars are double, as if two families had built together; some are distinctly marked; in others the stones have partly fallen in; all are more or less overgrown with lichens, and thick, short turf creeps everywhere in and about them. Sometimes garlands of woodbine drape the walls, and poison-ivy clasps and knots itself about the rocks; clumps of sweet flowering-elder cluster in the corners, or graceful, stag-horned sumachs, or raspberry bushes with ruddy fruit. Wild spiked thistles spread, and tall mullein-stalks stand like sentinels on guard over the desolation. Beautiful it is to see the delicate herb-robert's rosy

---

* "The character and habits of the original settlers for industry, intelligence, and pure morals have acquired for them great respect in the estimation of posterity." — *Williamson's History of Maine.*

flowers among the rough heaps of rocks, like a
tender afterthought where all is hard and stern.

It is a part of the religious belief of the Shoalers, that the ruinous cairn on the summit of Appledore was built by the famous John Smith and
his men when they discovered the islands in the
year 1614; and I will not be so heretical as to
doubt the fact, though it seems just as likely that
it was set up by fishermen and sailors as a land-
mark. At any rate, nobody knows when it was
not there, and it is perfectly safe to imagine any
origin for it. I never could be precisely certain
of the site of the first meeting-house on this isl-
and, "built (of brick) at a very early period, pos-
sibly the first in the province," says Williamson in
his "History of Maine." Probably there was no
cellar beneath it, and the slight underpinning has
been scattered and obliterated by time, — a fate
which many of the houses must have shared in like
manner. When man has vanished, Nature strives
to restore her original order of things, and she
smooths away gradually all traces of his work with
the broad hands of her changing seasons. The
men who built the Pyramids felt this; but will not
the world spin long enough to level their masonry
with the desolate sands? Neither is there any
sign of the foundation of that "Academy" to

which "even gentlemen from some of the principal towns on the sea-coast sent their sons for lit-
erary instruction," — I quote again from Williamson. How like a dream it seems, looking now at
these deserted rocks, that so much happened here
in the years that are gone! The connection of
Spain with these islands always had a great fascination for me; it is curious that the brightest and
gayest of lands, all aglow with sunshine and so
rich with southern beauty, should be in any way
linked with this place, so remote and desolate.
"In 1730, and afterwards, three or four ships used
to load at the Shoals with winter and spring merchantable fish for Bilboa in Spain." What wondrous craft must have navigated these waters, —
lazy, lumbering old ships, with quaintly carved fig-
ure-heads, and high-peaked sterns and prows, and
heavy draperies of weather-beaten sails, picturesque and charming to behold, and well enough
for the sparkling Mediterranean, but not the sort
of build to battle with the Atlantic breakers, as
several wrecks of vessels caught in the terrible
gales and driven upon the pitiless ledges might
testify! The ship Sagunto, it is said, met her destruction here as late as the year 1813; and there
are faint echoes of other disasters of the kind, but
the names of other ships have not come down to

2*   c

us. One wrecked on Appledore left only a quan-
tity of broad silver pieces sprinkled about the
rocks to tell of the calamity. A fisherman from
Star, paddling over in his dory to explore the coves
and chasms for driftwood (for the island was unin-
habited at the time), came suddenly upon the
glittering coins. His amazement was boundless.
After filling his pockets, a sudden terror possessed
him ; he began to have a suspicion that something
uncanny lurked at the bottom of such good fortune (for the superstition of the natives is very
great), and fled home to tell his neighbors, who
came in a body and made short work of the process
of gathering the rest of the treasure. Occasionally, since that time, coins have been found about
the southeast point, whereon the unknown vessel
struck and was completely destroyed. Of course
Captain Kidd, "as he sailed," is supposed to have
made the locality one of his many hiding-places.
I remember being awed when a child at the story
of how a certain old black Dinah, an inhabitant
of Portsmouth, came out to Appledore, then entirely divested of human abodes, and alone, with
only a divining-rod for company, passed several
days and nights wandering over the island, mut-
tering to herself, with her divining-rod carefully
balanced in her skinny hands. Robert Kidd's

buried treasure, if it existed, never signalled from below to that mystic rod, and the old negress returned empty-handed; but what a picture she must have made wandering there in the loneliness, by sunlight, or moonlight, or starlight, with her weird figure, her dark face, her garments fluttering in the wind, and the awful rod in her hand!

On Star Island, I have been told, a little three-legged black pot full of gold and silver pieces was dug up not very many years ago; and it is certainly true that Mr. Samuel Haley, who lived upon and owned Smutty-nose, in building a wall, turned over a large, flat stone beneath which lay four bars of solid silver. He must have been a fine, energetic old fellow, that Samuel Haley. With this treasure, says tradition again, he built, at great trouble and expense, the sea-wall which connects Smutty-nose with Malaga, and makes a safe harbor for distressed mariners in stormy weather. (This name Malaga, by the way, is a very distinct token of the Spaniards.) Not only did Haley build the sea-wall, but he erected salt-works which "manufactured excellent salt for the curing of fish," and stretched a ropewalk over the uneven ground to the extent of two hundred and seventy feet, and set up windmills to catch with their wide wings all the winds that blew, that he might grind his own corn and wheat, and live as independently as possible of his fellow-men ; for that is one of the first things a settler on the Isles of Shoals finds it necessary to learn. He planted a little orchard where the soil was deepest, and with much cherishing care contrived to coax his cherry-trees into abundant fruitfulness, and in every way made the most of the few advantages of the place. The old square house which he built upon his island, and which still stands, had, long ago, a broad balcony running the whole length of the house beneath the second-story windows. This being in a ruinous condition, I never dared venture out upon it ; but a large, square lookout, with a stout railing, which he built on the top of the house, remained till within a few years ; and I found it a charming place to linger in on still days, and watch the sky and the sea and the vessels, and the play of color over the bright face of the world. Looking from that airy station years ago, I used to think how many times he had sat there with his spy-glass, scanning the horizon and all within it, while the wind ruffled his gray hair and the sun shone pleasantly across his calm old face. Many years of his useful, happy life he lived there, and left behind him a beloved and honorable name. His descendants, still living upon Star, are among the best people in the village. A young girl bearing his name was lately married to one of the youthful fishermen. Star Island might well be proud of such a girl, so modest and sweet, and pretty too, slender and straight, dark-haired, brown-eyed, — as picturesque a creature as one would wish to see, with a delicate rose in her cheek and a clear light of intelligence in her eyes. Considering her, and remembering this ancient ancestor of hers, I thought she came honestly by her gentle, self-reliant expression, and her fine bearing, full of unconscious dignity and grace. The old man's quaint epitaph speaks of his humanity in "receiving into his enclosure many a poor, distressed seaman and fisherman in distress of weather." "In distress of weather!" One must live in such a place fully to comprehend the meaning of the words. It was his custom every night to put in his bedroom window, over the broad balcony facing the southeast, a light which burned all night, — a little act of thoughtfulness which speaks volumes. I think the lighthouse could not have been kindled at that time, but I am not sure. There is much uncertainty with regard to dates and records of those old times. Mr. Haley is said to have died in 1811, but I have always heard that he was living when the Sagunto was wrecked upon his island, which happened, according to the Gosport records, in 1813. This is the entry: "Ship Sagunto stranded on Smotinose Isle Jany 14th 1813 Jany 15th one man found, Jany 16th 6 men found 21 – 7 the Number of men yet found Belonging to said ship twelve." I am inclined to think the writer made a mistake in his date as well as his spelling and arithmetic, for it is an accepted tradition that Mr. Haley found and buried the dead crew of that ship, and I have always heard it spoken of as a simple fact. On that stormy January night, runs the story, he placed the light as usual in his chamber window, and I dare say prayed in his good heart that no vessel might be wandering near this dangerous place, tossed helpless on the raging sea in the thick darkness and bitter cold and blinding snow. But that night the great ship Sagunto drove, crashing, full upon the fatal southeast point, in sight of the tiny spark that burned peacefully, unwavering, in that quiet chamber. Her costly timbers of mahogany and cedar-wood were splintered on the sharp teeth of those inexorable rocks; her cargo of dried fruits and nuts and bales of broadcloth and gold and silver, was tossed about the shore, and part of her crew were thrown alive upon it. Some of them saw the light, and crawled

toward it benumbed with cold and spent with
fatigue and terror. The roaring of the storm
bore away their faint cries of distress; the old
man slept on quietly, with his family about him,
sheltered, safe; while a stone's-throw from his
door these sailors strove and agonized to reach
that friendly light. Two of them gained the stone-
wall in front of the house, but their ebbing strength
would not allow them to climb over; they threw
themselves upon it, and perished miserably, with
safety, warmth, and comfort so close at hand! In
the morning, when the tumult was somewhat
hushed, and underneath the sullen sky rolled the
more sullen sea in long, deliberate waves, the old
man looked out in the early light across the waste
of snow, and on the wall lay — something that
broke the familiar outline, though all was smooth
with the pure, soft snow. He must put on coat
and cap, and go and find out what this strange
thing might be. Ah, that was a sight for his pity-
ing eyes under the cold and leaden light of that
unrelenting morning! He summoned his sons
and his men. Quickly the alarm was given, and
there was confusion and excitement as the islanders, hurriedly gathering, tried if it were possible
yet to save some life amid the wreck. But it was
too late; every soul was lost. Fourteen bodies

were found at that time, strewn all the way between the wall and that southeast point where the vessel had gone to pieces. The following summer the skeleton of another was discovered among some bushes near the shore. The imagination lingers over those poor drowned sailors ; strives to figure what each man was like, what might have been the musical name of each (for all names in Spanish should be musical, with a reminiscence of flute and guitar in them) ; dwells on the dark-olive faces and jet-black hair, the graceful foreign dress, — curious short jackets, perhaps, with bits of bright embroidery that loving hands had worked for them, all stained and tarnished by the brine. No doubt some of them wore about their necks a cross or amulet, with an image of the " Blessed Virgin " or the " Son of God," that so they might be saved from just such a fate as this ; and maybe some one among these sailor-men carried against his heart a lock of hair, dark and lustrous before the washing of the cold waves dulled the brightness of its beauty. Fourteen shallow graves were quarried for the unknown dead in the iron earth, and there they lie, with him who buried them a little above in the same grassy slope. Here is his epitaph : —

" In memory of Mr. Samuel Haley
Who died in the year 1811
Aged 84
He was a man of great Ingenuity
Industry Honor and Honesty, true to his
Country & A man who did A great
Publik good in Building A
Dock & Receiving into his
Enclosure many a poor
Distressed Seaman & Fisherman
In distress of Weather."

A few steps from their resting-place the low wall on which the two unfortunates were found frozen is falling into ruin. The glossy green leaves of the bayberry-bushes crowd here and there about it, in odorous ranks on either side, and sweetly the warm blush of the wild-rose glows against its cool gray stones. Leaning upon it in summer afternoons, when the wind is quiet and there steals up a fragrance and fresh murmur from the incoming tide, when the slowly mellowing light lies tranquil over the placid sea, enriching everything it touches with infinite beauty, — waves and rocks that kill and destroy, blossoming roses and lonely graves, — a wistful sadness colors all one's thoughts. Afar off the lazy waters sing and smile about that white point, shimmering in the brilliant atmosphere. How peaceful it is! How innocent and unconscious is the whole face of this awful and beautiful nature! But, listening to the blissful murmur of the tide, one can but think with what another voice that tide spoke when it ground the ship to atoms and roared with sullen thunder about those dying men.

There is no inscription on the rough boulders at the head and foot of these graves. A few more years, and all trace of them will be obliterated. Already the stones lean this way and that, and are half buried in the rank grass. Soon will they be entirely forgotten; the old, old world forgets so much! And it is sown thick with graves from pole to pole.

"These islands bore some of the first footprints of New-England Christianity and civilization. They were for a long time the abode of intelligence, refinement, and virtue, but were afterwards abandoned to a state of semi-barbarism." The first intelligence of the place comes to us from the year 1614, when John Smith is supposed to have discovered them. The next date is of the landing of Christopher Leavitt, in 1623. In 1645, three brothers, Robert, John, and Richard Cutts, emigrated from Wales, and on their way to the continent paused at the Isles of Shoals, and, finding them so pleasant, made their settlement here. Williamson mentions particularly Richard Gibson, from Topsham, England, and various other men from England and Wales. Many people speedily joined the little colony, which grew yearly more prosperous. In 1650, the Rev. John Brock came to live among the islanders, and remained with them twelve years. All that we hear of this man is so fine, he is represented as having been so faithful, zealous, intelligent, and humane, that it is no wonder the community flourished while he sat at the helm. It was said of him, " He dwells as near Heaven as any man upon earth." Cotton Mather thus quaintly praises him : " He was a good *grammarian,* chiefly in this, that he still *spoke the truth from his heart.* He was a good *logician,* chiefly in this, that he *presented himself unto God with a reasonable service.* He was a good *arith-metician,* chiefly in this, that he *so numbered his days as to apply his heart unto wisdom.* He was a good *astronomer,* chiefly in this, *that his conversation was in Heaven.* . . . . So much belonged to this *good man,* that so *learned a life* may well be judged worthy of being a *written one.*" After him came a long procession of the clergy, good, bad, and indifferent, up to the present time, when "divine service," so-called, has seemed a mere burlesque as it has been often carried on in the little church at Star.

Last summer I was shown a quaint little book entitled "The Fisherman's Calling. A brief essay to Serve the Great Interests of Religion among our Fishermen. By Cotton Mather, D. D. Boston in New England. Printed : Sold by T. Green. 1712," and I found the following incident connected with Mr. Brock's ministry at the Shoals : " To Illustrate and Demonstrate the Providence of God our Saviour over the Business of fishermen, I will entertain you with Two short Modern Histories." Then follows an account of some Romish priests upon some isles belonging to Scotland, who endeavored to draw the poor fishermen over to popery. The other is this : " When our Mr. Brock lived on the Isles of Shoals, he brought the Fishermen into an agreement that besides the Lord's Day they would spend one day of every month together in the worship of the Glorious Lord. A certain day which by their Agreement belonged unto the Exercises of Religion being arrived, they came to Mr. Brock, and asked him, that they might put by their meeting and go a Fishing, because they had Lost many Days by the Foulness of the weather. He, seeing that without and against his consent they resolved upon doing what they asked of him, replied, ' If you will go away I say unto you, ' Catch Fish if you can ! ' But as for you that will tarry, and worship our Lord

Jesus Christ this day, I will pray unto Him for you that you may afterwards take fish till you are weary.' Thirty men went away from the meeting and Five tarried. The thirty that went away from the meeting with all their Craft could catch but four Fishes. The Five which tarried went forth afterwards and *they* took *five Hundred*. The Fishermen were after this Readier to hearken unto the Voice of their Teacher."

If virtue were often its own reward after a fashion like this, in what a well-conducted world we should live! Doubtless the reckless islanders needed the force of all the moral suasion good Mr. Brock could bring to bear upon them; too much law and order they could not have; but I like better this story of the stout old fisherman who in church so unexpectedly answered his pastor's thrilling exhortation, "Supposing, my brethren, that any of you should be overtaken in the bay by a northeast storm, your hearts trembling with fear, and nothing but death before, whither would your thoughts turn? what would you do?" — with the instant inspiration of common-sense, "I'd hoist the foresail and scud away for Squam!"

The first church on Star was built principally of timbers from the wrecks of Spanish ships, but it has been partially burned and rebuilt twice.

Various rough characters, given over to hard drinking, and consequently lawless living, have joined the colony within the last ten years, and made the place the scene of continually recurring fires. On going down to Appledore one spring I was surprised at the daily and nightly jangling of the dull bell at Star, —a dissonant sound borne wildly on the stormy wind to our dwelling. " What is Star Island ringing for ? " I kept asking, and was as often answered, " O, it 's only Sam Blake setting his house on fire ! " — the object being to obtain the insurance thereupon.

On the Massachusetts records there is a paragraph to the effect that, in the year 1653, Philip Babb, of Hog Island, was appointed constable for all the islands of Shoals, Star Island excepted. To Philip Babb we shall have occasion to refer again. "In May, 1661," says Williamson, "being places of note and great resort, the General Court incorporated the islands into a town called Appledore, and invested it with the powers and privileges of other towns." There were then about forty families on Hog Island, but between that time and the year 1670 these removed to Star Island and joined the settlement there. This they were induced to do partly through fear of the Indians, who frequented Duck Island, and thence made plundering excursions upon them, carrying off their women while they were absent fishing, and doing a variety of harm ; but, as it is expressly stated that people living on the mainland sent their children to school at Appledore that they might be safe from the Indians, the statement of their depredations at the Shoals is perplexing. Probably the savages camped on Duck to carry on their craft of porpoise-fishing, which to this day they still pursue among the islands on the eastern coast of Maine. Star Island seemed a place of greater safety; and probably the greater advantages of landing and the convenience of a wide cove at the entrance of the village, with a little harbor wherein the fishing-craft might anchor with some security, were also inducements. William Pepperell, a native of Cornwall, England, emigrated to the place in the year 1676, and lived there upwards of twenty years, and carried on a large fishery. "He was the father of Sir William Pepperell, the most famous man Maine ever produced." For more than a century previous to the Revolutionary War there were at the Shoals from three to six hundred inhabitants, and the little settlement flourished steadily. They had their church and school-house, and a court-house; and the usual municipal officers were annually chosen, and the

town records regularly kept.   From three to four
thousand quintals of fish were yearly caught and
cured by the islanders ; and, beside their trade
with Spain, large quantities of fish were also carried to Portsmouth, for the West India market.
In 1671 the islands belonged to John Mason and
Sir Ferdinando Gorges.   This man always greatly
interested me.   He must have been a person of
great force of character, strong, clear-headed, full
of fire and energy.   He was appointed governor-
general of New England in 1637.   Williamson has
much to say of him : " He and Sir Walter Raleigh,
whose acquaintance was familiar, possessing minds
equally elastic and adventurous, turned their
thoughts at an early period of life towards the
American hemisphere."   And the historian thus
goes on lamenting over him : " Fame and wealth,
so often the idols of superior intellects, were the
prominent objects of this aspiring man.   Constant
and sincere in his friendships, he might have had
extensively the estimation of others, had not self-
ishness been the centre of all his efforts.   His life
and name, though by no means free from blem-
ishes, have just claims to the grateful recollections
of the Eastern Americans and their posterity."

From 1640 to 1775, says a report to the "Society for Propagating the Gospel among the Indians

and Others in North America," the church at the Shoals was in a flourishing condition, and had a succession of ministers, — Messrs. Hull, Brock, Belcher, Moody, Tucke, and Shaw, all of whom were good and faithful men; two, Brock and Tucke, being men of learning and ability, with peculiarities of talent and character admirably fitting them for their work on these islands. Tucke was the only one who closed his life and ministry at the Shoals. He was a graduate of Harvard College of the class of 1723, was ordained at the Shoals July 20, 1732, and died there August 12, 1773, — his ministry thus covering more than forty years. His salary in 1771 was paid in merchantable fish, a quintal to a man, when there were on the Shoals from ninety to one hundred men, and a quintal of fish was worth a guinea. His grave was accidentally discovered in 1800, and the Hon. Dudley Atkins Tyng, who interested himself most charitably and indefatigably for the good of these islands, placed over it a slab of stone, with an inscription which still remains to tell of the fine qualities of the man whose dust it covers; but year by year the raindrops with delicate touches wear away the deeply cut letters, for the stone lies horizontal; even now they are scarcely legible, and soon the words of praise and appreciation, will exist only in the memory of a few of the older inhabitants.

At the time of Mr. Tucke's death the prosperity of the Shoals was at its height. But in less than thirty years after his death a most woful condition of things was inaugurated.

The settlement flourished till the breaking out of the war, when it was found to be entirely at the mercy of the English, and obliged to furnish them with recruits and supplies. The inhabitants were therefore ordered by the government to quit the islands; and as their trade was probably broken up and their property exposed, most of them complied with the order, and settled in the neighboring seaport towns, where their descendants may be found to this day. Some of the people settled in Salem, and the Mr. White so mysteriously murdered there many years ago was born at Appledore. Those who remained, with a few exceptions, were among the most ignorant and degraded of the people, and they went rapidly down into untold depths of misery. "They burned the meeting-house, and gave themselves up to quarrelling, profanity, and drunkenness, till they became almost barbarians"; or, as Mr. Morse expresses it, "were given up to work all manner of wickedness with greediness." In no place of the size has there been a greater absorption of "rum" since the world was made. Mr. Reuben Moody, a theological student, lived at the Shoals for a few months in the year 1822, and his description of the condition of things at that time is frightful. He had no place to open a school; one of the islanders provided him with a room, fire, etc., giving as a reason for his enthusiastic furtherance of Mr. Moody's plans, that his children made such a disturbance at home that he couldn't sleep in the daytime. An extract from Mr. Moody's journal affords an idea of the morals of the inhabitants at this period : —

"May 1st. I yet continue to witness the Heaven-daring impieties of this people. Yesterday my heart was shocked at seeing a man about seventy years of age, as devoid of reason as a maniac, giving way to his passions ; striving to express himself in more blasphemous language than he had the ability to utter; and, being unable to express the malice of his heart in words, he would *run at* every one he saw. All was tumult and confusion, — men and women with tar-brushes, clenched fists, and stones ; one female who had an infant but eight days old, with a stone in her hand and an oath on her tongue, threatened to dash out the brains of her antagonists. . . . . After I arrived among them some of them dispersed, some led their wives into the house, others drove them off, and a calm succeeded."

In another part of the journal is an account of an old man who lived alone and drank forty gallons of rum in twelve months, — some horrible old Caliban, no doubt. This hideous madness of drunkenness was the great trouble at the Shoals; and though time has modified, it has not eliminated the apparently hereditary bane whose antidote is not yet discovered. The misuse of strong drink still proves a whirlpool more awful than the worst terrors of the pitiless ocean that hems the islanders in.

As may be seen from Mr. Moody's journal, the clergy had a hard time of it among the heathen at the Isles of Shoals ; but they persevered, and many brave women at different times have gone among the people to teach the school and reclaim the little children from wretchedness and ignorance. Miss Peabody, of Newburyport, who came to live with them in 1823, did wonders for them during the three years of her stay. She taught the school, visited the families, and on Sundays read to such audiences as she could collect, took seven of the poorer female children to live with her at the parsonage, instructed all who would learn in the arts of carding, spinning, weaving, knitting, sewing, braiding mats, etc. Truly she remembered what "Satan finds for idle hands to do," and kept all her charges busy and consequently happy. All honor to her memory! she was a wise and faithful servant. There is still an affectionate remembrance of her among the present inhabitants, whose mothers she helped out of their degradation into a better life. I saw in one of the houses, not long ago, a sampler blackened by age, but carefully preserved in a frame; and was told that the dead grandmother of the family had made it when a little girl, under Miss Peabody's supervision. In 1835 the Rev. Origen Smith went to live at Star, and remained perhaps ten years, doing much good among the people. He nearly succeeded in banishing the great demoralizer, liquor, and restored law and order. He is reverently remembered by the islanders. In 1855 an excellent man by the name of Mason occupied the post of minister for the islanders, and from his report to the "Society for Propagating the Gospel among the Indians and Others in North America" I make a few extracts. He says: "The kind of business which the people pursue, and by which they subsist, affects unfavorably their habits, physical, social, and religious. Family discipline is neglected, domestic arrange-

ments very imperfect, much time, apparently
wasted, is spent in watching for favorable indica-
tions to pursue their calling. . . . . A bad moral
influence is excited by a portion of the transient
visitors to the Shoals during the summer months."
This is very true. He speaks of the people's appreciation of the efforts made in their behalf; and
says that they raised subscriptions among themselves for lighting the parsonage, and for fuel for
the singing-school (which, by the way, was a most
excellent institution), and mentions their surprising
him by putting into the back kitchen of the parsonage a barrel of fine flour, a bucket of sugar, a
leg of bacon, etc. "Their deep poverty abounded
unto the riches of their liberality," he says; and
this little act shows that they were far from being
indifferent or ungrateful. They were really attached to Mr. Mason, and it is a pity he could not
have remained with them.

Within the last few years they have been trying
bravely to help themselves, and they persevere
with their annual fair to obtain money to pay the
teacher who saves their little children from utter
ignorance; and many of them show a growing
ambition in fitting up their houses and making
their families more comfortable. Of late, the fires
before referred to, kindled in drunken madness by

the islanders themselves, or by the reckless few
who have joined the settlement, have swept away
nearly all the old houses, which have been re-
placed by smart new buildings, painted white,
with green blinds, and with modern improvements,
so that yearly the village grows less picturesque, —
which is a charm one can afford to lose, when the
external smartness is indicative of better living
among the people. Twenty years ago Star Island
Cove was charming, with its tumble-down fish-
houses, and ancient cottages with low, shelving
roofs, and porches covered with the golden lichen
that so loves to embroider old weather-worn wood.
Now there is not a vestige of those dilapidated
buildings to be seen; almost everything is white
and square and new; and they have even cleaned
out the cove, and removed the great accumulation
of fish-bones which made the beach so curious.

The old town records are quaint and interesting, and the spelling and modes of expression so
peculiar that I have copied a few. Mr. John
Muchamore was the moderator of a meeting called
" March ye 7th day, 1748. By a Legall town
meeting of ye Free holders and Inhabitence of
gosport, dewly quallefide to vote for Tiding men
Collerc of fish, Corders of wood. Addition to ye
minister's sallery Mr John Tucke, 100 lbs old
tenor."

In 1755, it was " Agred in town meating **that if** any person shall spelth [split] any fish above hie water marck and leave their heads and son bones [sound-bones] their, shall pay ten lbs new tenor to the town, and any that is above now their, they that have them their, shall have them below hie warter in fortinets time or pay the same." In another place " it is agreed at ton meating evry person that is are kow [has a cow] shall carry them of at 15 day of may, keep them their til the 15 day of October or pay 20 shillings lawful money." And " if any person that have any hogs, If they do any damg, hom [whom] they do the damg to shall keep the hog for sattisfaxeon."

The cows seem to have given a great deal of trouble. Here is one more extract on the subject : —

" This is a Leagel vot by the ton meeting, that if any presson or pressons shall leave their Cowks out after the fifteenth day of May and they do any Dameg, they shall be taken up and the owner of the kow shall pay teen shillings old tenor to the kow constabel and one half he shall have and the other shall give to the pour of the place.

" Mr Dainel Randel
" *Kow Constabel.*"

" On March 11th 1762. A genarel free Voot

Gosport harbor with Smuttynose island at right and Appledore island at left.

The village of Gosport, Star island, prior to 1871.

Important Gosport buildings included, the church, left, the school, center, and the parsonage, right. Only the church remains.

The Gosport school and students.

past amongst the inhabents that every fall of the year when Mr Rev^d· John Tucke has his wood to Carry home evary men will not com that is abel to com shall pay forty shillings ould tenor."

But the most delightfully preposterous entry is this : —

"March 12th 1769. A genarel free voot past amongst the inhabents to cus [cause] tow men to go to the Rev^d Mr John Tucke to hear wether he was willing to take one Quental of fish each man, or to take the price of Quental in ould tenor which he answered this that he thought it was easer to pay the fish than the money which he consented to taik the fish for the year insuing."

"On March ye 25 1771. "then their was a meating called and it was *gurned* until the 23rd day of apirel.

"Mr Deeken Willam Muchmore
"*Moderator.*"

Among the "offorsers" of "Gospored" were, besides "Moderator" and "Town Clarke," "Seelekt meen," "Counstauble," "Tidon meen" (Tithing-men), "Coulears of fish," — "Coulear" meaning, I suppose, culler, or person appointed to select fish, — and "Sealers of Whood," oftener expressed corders of wood.

3*

In 1845 we read that Asa Caswell was chosen highway " sovair."

Very ancient tradition says that the method of courtship at the Isles of Shoals was after this fashion : If a youth fell in love with a maid, he lay in wait till she passed by, and then pelted her with stones, after the manner of our friends of Marblehead ; so that if a fair Shoaler found herself the centre of a volley of missiles, she might be sure that an ardent admirer was expressing himself with decision certainly, if not with tact ! If she turned, and exhibited any curiosity as to the point of the compass whence the bombardment proceeded, her doubts were dispelled by another shower ; but if she went on her way in maiden meditation, then was her swain in despair, and life, as is usual in such cases, became a burden to him.

Within my remembrance an occasional cabbage-party made an agreeable variety in the life of the villagers. I never saw one, but have heard them described. Instead of regaling the guests with wine and ices, pork and cabbage were the principal refreshments offered them ; and if the cabbage came out of the garden of a neighbor, the spice of wickedness lent zest to the entertainment, — stolen fruit being always the sweetest.

It would seem strange that, while they live in

so healthy a place, where the atmosphere is absolutely perfect in its purity, they should have suffered so much from ill health, and that so many
should have died of consumption, — the very dis-
ease for the cure of which physicians send invalids
hither. The reasons are soon told. The first
and most important is this: that, as nearly as they
could, they have in past years hermetically sealed
their houses, so that the air of heaven should not
penetrate within. An open window, especially at
night, they would have looked upon as madness, —
a temptation of Providence ; and during the winter
they have deliberately poisoned themselves with
every breath, like two thirds of the rest of the
world. I have seen a little room containing a
whole family, fishing-boots and all, bed, furniture,
cooking-stove in full blast, and an oil lamp with a
wick so high that the deadly smoke rose steadily,
filling the air with what Browning might call
" filthiest gloom," and mingling with the incense
of ancient tobacco-pipes smoked by both sexes
(for nearly all the old women used to smoke) ;
every crack and cranny was stopped ; and if, by
any chance, the door opened for an instant, out
rushed a fume in comparison with which the gusts
from the lake of Tartarus might be imagined
sweet. Shut in that deadly air, a part of the

family slept, sometimes all. What wonder that
their chests were hollow, their faces haggard, and
that apathy settled upon them! Then their food
was hardly selected with reference to health, sal-
eratus and pork forming two of the principal in-
gredients in their daily fare. Within a few years
past they have probably improved in these re-
spects. Fifteen years ago I was passing a window
one morning, at which a little child two years old
was sitting, tied into a high chair before a table
drawn close to the window, eating his breakfast
alone in his glory. In his stout little fist he
grasped a large iron spoon, and fed himself from
a plate of beans swimming in fat, and with the
pork cut up in squares for his better convenience.
By the side of the plate stood a tin mug of bitter-
strong black coffee sweetened with molasses. I
spoke to his mother within; "Ar' n't you afraid
such strong coffee will kill your baby?" "O no,"
she answered, and held it to his lips. "There,
drink that," she said, "that 'll make you hold
your head up!" The poor child died before he
grew to be a man, and all the family have fallen
victims to consumption.

Very few of the old people are left at the present time, and the village is very like other fishing-
villages along the coast. Most of the peculiar

characteristics of the race are lost in the present generation of young women, who are addicted to the use of hoops and water-falls, and young men, who condescend to spoil their good looks by dyeing their handsome blond beards with the fashionable mixture which inevitably produces a lustre like stove-blacking. But there are sensible fellows among them, fine specimens of the hardy New England fisherman, Saxon-bearded, broad-shouldered, deep-chested, and bronzed with shade on shade of ruddy brown. The neutral blues and grays of the salt-water make perfect backgrounds for the pictures these men are continually showing one in their life about the boats. Nothing can be more satisfactory than the blendings and contrasts of color and the picturesque effect of the general aspect of the natives in their element. The eye is often struck with the richness of the color of some rough hand, glowing with mingled red, brown, and orange, against the gray-blue water, as it grasps an oar, perhaps, or pulls in a rope. It is strange that the sun and wind, which give such fine tints to the complexions of the lords of creation, should leave such hideous traces on the faces of women. When they are exposed to the same salt wind and clear sunshine they take the hue of dried fish, and become objects for men and

angels to weep over.   To see a *bona fide* Shoaler
" sail a boat " (when the craft is a real boat and
no tub) is an experience.   The vessel obeys his
hand at the rudder as a trained horse a touch on
the rein, and seems to bow at the flash of his
eye, turning on her heel and running up into the
wind, "luffing " to lean again on the other tack, —
obedient, graceful, perfectly beautiful, yielding to
breeze and to billow, yet swayed throughout by a
stronger and more imperative law.   The men become strongly attached to their boats, which seem
to have a sort of human interest for them, — and
no wonder.   They lead a life of the greatest hard-
ship and exposure, during the winter especially,
setting their trawls fifteen or twenty miles to the
eastward of the islands, drawing them next day if
the stormy winds and waves will permit, and taking the fish to Portsmouth to sell.   It is desperately hard work, trawling at this season, with the
bitter wind blowing in their teeth, and the flying
spray freezing upon everything it touches, —
boats, masts, sails, decks, clothes completely cased
in ice, and fish frozen solid as soon as taken from
the water.   The inborn politeness of these fishermen to stranger-women is something delightful to
witness.   I remember once landing in Portsmouth,
and being obliged to cross three or four schooners

just in (with their freight of frozen fish lying open-mouthed in a solid mass on deck) to reach the wharf. No courtly gentlemen could have displayed more beautiful behavior than did these rough fellows, all pressing forward, with real grace, — because the feeling which prompted them was a true and lofty feeling, — to help me over the tangle of ropes and sails and anchors to a safe footing on shore. There is a ledge forty-five miles east of the islands, called Jeffrey's Ledge, where the Shoalers go for spring fishing. During a northeast storm in May, part of the little fleet came reeling in before the gale; and, not daring to trust themselves to beat up into the harbor (a poor shelter at best), round the rocky reefs and ledges, the fishermen anchored under the lee of Appledore, and there rode out the storm. They were in continual peril; for, had their cables chafed apart with the shock and strain of the billows among which they plunged, or had their anchors dragged (which might have been expected, the bottom of the sea between the islands and the mainland being composed of mud, while all outside is rough and rocky), they would have inevitably been driven to their destruction on the opposite coast. It was not pleasant to watch them as the early twilight shut down over the

vast, weltering desolation of the sea, to see the
slender masts waving helplessly from one side to
another, — sometimes almost horizontal, as the
hulls turned heavily this way and that, and the
long breakers rolled in endless succession against
them. They saw the lights in our windows a half-
mile away; and we, in the warm, bright, quiet room,
sitting by a fire that danced and shone, fed with
bits of wreck such as they might scatter on Rye
Beach before morning, could hardly think of anything else than the misery of those poor fellows,
wet, cold, hungry, sleepless, full of anxiety till
the morning should break and the wind should
lull. No boat could reach them through the terrible commotion of waves. But they rode through
the night in safety, and the morning brought relief. One brave little schooner " toughed it out "
on the distant ledge, and her captain told me that
no one could stand on board of her; the pressure
of the wind down on her decks was so great that
she shuddered from stem to stern, and he feared
she would shake to pieces, for she was old and not
very seaworthy. Some of the men had wives and
children watching them from lighted windows at
Star. What a fearful night for them ! They could
not tell from hour to hour, through the thick
darkness, if yet the cables held; they could not

see till daybreak whether the sea had swallowed up their treasures. I wonder the wives were not white-haired when the sun rose, and showed them those little specks yet rolling in the breakers! The women are excessively timid about the water, more so than landswomen. Having the terror and might of the ocean continually encircling them, they become more impressed with it and distrust it, knowing it so well. Very few accidents happen, however : the islanders are a cautious people. Years ago, when the white sails of their little fleet of whale-boats used to flutter out of the sheltered bight and stand out to the fishing-grounds in the bay, how many eyes followed them in the early light, and watched them in the distance through the day, till, toward sunset, they spread their wings to fly back with the evening wind! How pathetic the gathering of women on the headlands, when out of the sky swept the squall that sent the small boats staggering before it, and blinded the eyes, already drowned in tears, with sudden rain that hid sky and sea and boats from their eager gaze! What wringing of hands, what despairing cries, which the wild wind bore away while it caught and fluttered the homely draperies and unfastened the locks of maid and mother, to blow them about their pale faces and anxious eyes!

E

Now no longer the little fleet goes forth; for the greater part of the islanders have stout schooners, and go trawling with profit, if not with pleasure. A few solitaries fish in small dories and earn a slender livelihood thereby.

The sea helps these poor people by bringing fuel to their very doors; the waves continually deposit driftwood in every fissure of the rocks. But sad, anxious lives they have led, especially the women, many of whom have grown old before their time with hard work and bitter cares, with hewing of wood and drawing of water, turning of fish on the flakes to dry in the sun, endless household work, and the cares of maternity, while their lords lounged about the rocks in their scarlet shirts in the sun, or "held up the walls of the meeting-house," as one expressed it, with their brawny shoulders. I never saw such wrecks of humanity as some of the old women of Star Island, who have long since gone to their rest. In my childhood I caught glimpses of them occasionally, their lean brown shapes crouching over the fire, with black pipes in their sunken mouths, and hollow eyes, "of no use now but to gather brine," and rough, gray, straggling locks: despoiled and hopeless visions, it seemed as if youth and joy could never have been theirs.

A WOMAN OF STAR ISLAND.

ISLES OF SHOALS, 1844.

OVER the embers she sits,
   Close at the edge of the grave,
With her hollow eyes like pits,
   And her mouth like a sunken cave.

Her short black pipe held tight
   Her withered lips between,
She rocks in the flickering light
   Her figure bent and lean.

She turns the fish no more
   That dry on the flakes in the sun;
No wood she drags to the door,
   Nor water, — her labor is done.

She cares not for oath or blow,
   She is past all hope or fear ;
There is nothing she cares to know,
   There is nothing hateful or dear.

Deep wrong have the bitter years
   Wrought her, both body and soul.
Life has been seasoned with tears;
   But saw not God the whole?

O wreck in woman's shape!
   Were you ever gracious and sweet?
Did youth's enchantment drape
   This horror, from head to feet?

Have dewy eyes looked out
   From these hollow pits forlorn?
Played smiles the mouth about
   Of shy, still rapture born?

Yea, once.   But long ago
　　Has evil ground away
All beauty.   The salt winds blow
　　On no sorrier sight to-day.

Trodden utterly out
　　Is every spark of hope.
There is only left her, a doubt,
　　A gesture, half-conscious, a grope

In the awful dark for a Touch
　　That never yet failed a soul.
Is not God tender to such?
　　Hath he not seen the whole?

The local pronunciation of the Shoalers is very peculiar, and a shrewd sense of humor is one of their leading characteristics.   Could De Quincey have lived among them, I think he might have been tempted to write an essay on swearing as a fine art, for it has reached a pitch hardly short of sublimity in this favored spot.   They seemed to have a genius for it, and some of them really devoted their best powers to its cultivation.   The language was taxed to furnish them with prodigious forms of speech wherewith to express the slightest emotion of pain, anger, or amusement ; and though the blood of the listener was sometimes chilled in his veins, overhearing their unhesitating profanity, the prevailing sentiment was likely to be one of amazement mingled with intense amusement, —

the whole thing was so grotesque and monstrous, and their choice of words so comical, and generally so very much to the point.

The real Shoals phraseology existing in past years was something not to be described; it is impossible by any process known to science to convey an idea of the intonations of their speech, quite different from Yankee drawl or sailor-talk, and perfectly unique in itself. Why they should have called a swallow a "swallick" and a sparrow a "sparrick" I never could understand; or what they mean by calling a great gale or tempest a "Tan toaster." Anything that ends in *y* or *e* they still pronounce *ay* with great breadth; for instance, "Benny" is Bennaye; "Billy" Billay, and so on. A man by the name of Beebe, the modern "missionary," was always spoken of as Beebay, when he was not called by a less respectful title. Their sense of fun showed itself in the nicknames with which they designated any person possessing the slightest peculiarity. For instance, twenty years ago a minister of the Methodist persuasion came to live among them; his wife was unreasonably tall and thin. With the utmost promptitude and decision the irreverent christened her "Legs," and never spoke of her by any other name. "Laigs has gone to Portsmouth," or "Laigs has got a

new gown," etc.   A spinster of very dark com-
plexion was called "Scip," an abbreviation of
Scipio, a name supposed to appertain particularly
to the colored race.   Another was called "Squint,"
because of a defect in the power of vision ; and
not only were they spoken of by these names,
but called so to their faces habitually.   One man
earned for himself the title of "Brag," so that
no one ever thought of calling him by his real
name ; his wife was Mrs. Brag ; and constant use
so robbed these names of their offensiveness that
the bearers not only heard them with equanimity,
but would hardly have known themselves by their
true ones.   A most worthy Norwegian took up his
abode for a brief space among them a few years
ago.   His name was Ingebertsen.   Now, to expect
any Shoaler would trouble himself to utter such
a name as that was beyond all reason.   At once
they called him "Carpenter," apropos of nothing
at all, for he never had been a carpenter.   But
the name was the first that occurred to them, and
sufficiently easy of utterance.   It was "Carpenter," and "Mis' Carpenter," and "them Carpenter
children," and the name still clings to fine old
Ingebertsen and his family.   Grandparents are
addressed as Grans and Gwammaye, Grans being
an abbreviation of grandsire.   " Tell yer grans

his dinner's ready," calls some woman from a cot
tage door. One old man, too lazy almost to live,
was called "Hing"; one of two brothers "Bunker,"
the other "Shothead"; an ancient scold was called
"Zeke," another "Sir Polly," and so on indefi-
nitely. In pleasant weather sometimes the younger
women would paddle from one island to another
"making calls." If any old "Grans" perceived
them, loafing at his door in the sun, "It's going
to storm! the women begin to flit!" he would
cry, as if they were a flock of coots. A woman,
describing how slightly her house was put together,
said, "Lor', 't wan't never built, 't was only hove together." "I don' know whe'r or no it's best or no
to go fishin' whiles mornin'," says some rough fellow, meditating upon the state of winds and waters.
Of his boat another says with pride, "*She's* a
pretty piece of wood!" and another, "She strikes
a sea and comes down like a pillow," describing
her smooth sailing. Some one, relating the way
the civil authorities used to take political matters
into their own hands, said that "if a man did n't
vote as they wanted him to, they took him and
hove him up agin the meetin' us," by way of bringing him to his senses. Two boys in bitter conten-
tion have been heard calling each other "nasty-
faced chowderheads," as if the force of language

could no further go. " I 'm dryer than a graven image," a man says when he is thirsty. But it is impossible to give an idea of their common speech leaving out the profanity which makes it so startling.

Some comical stories are told of the behavior of officers of the law in certain emergencies. On one occasion two men attacked each other in the cove which served as the Plaza, the grand square of the village, the general lounging-place. A comrade in a state of excitement ran to inform the one policeman, who straightway repaired to the scene of battle. There were the combatants raging like wild beasts, while the whole community looked on aghast. What was to be done? Evidently something, and at once. The policeman looked about him, considering. As for interfering with that fearful twain, it was out of the question. His eye fell upon a poor old man who leaned against a fish-house enjoying the scene. A happy thought struck him! He dashed down upon the ancient and unoffending spectator, and hurled him to the ground with such force that he broke his collar-bone. Then, I suppose, he retired, serene in the proud consciousness of having done his duty, and of having been fully equal to the occasion.

Two of the chief magistrates of the place had a deadly feud, entirely personal, which had smouldered between them for years. One day the stronger of the two quietly " arrested " the weaker, tied him hand and foot with ropes, "hove" him into his whale-boat, and sailed off with him in triumph to the land. Arrived at the city of Portsmouth, he conducted him to jail, delivered him over to the jailer with much satisfaction, crying, " There ! There he is ! Take him and lock him up ! He 's a poor pris'ner. Don't you give him nothin' t' eat ! " and returned rejoicing to the bosom of his family. It being Thanksgiving Day, the jailer is said to have taken the prisoner at once into his house, and, instead of locking him up, gave him, according to his own account, " one of the best Thanksgiving dinners he ever ate."

Nearly all the Shoalers have a singular gait, contracted from the effort to keep their equilibrium while standing in boats, and from the unavoidable gymnastics which any attempt at locomotion among the rocks renders necessary. Some stiff-jointed old men have been known to leap wildly from broad stone to stone on the smooth, flat pavements of Portsmouth town, finding it out of the question to walk evenly and decorously along the straight and easy way. This is no fable.

4

Such is the force of habit. Most of the men are more or less round-shouldered, and seldom row upright, with head erect and shoulders thrown back. They stoop so much over the fish-tables — cleaning, splitting, salting, packing — that they acquire a permanent habit of stooping.

Twenty years ago, an old man by the name of Peter was alive on Star Island. He was said to be a hundred years old ; and anything more grisly, in the shape of humanity, it has never been my lot to behold ; so lean and brown and ancient, he might have been Methuselah, for no one knew how long he had lived on this rolling planet. Years before he died he used to paddle across to our lighthouse, in placid summer days, and, scanning him with a child's curiosity, I wondered how he kept alive. A few white hairs clung to his yellow crown, and his pale eyes, " where the very blue had turned to white," looked vacantly and wearily out, as if trying faintly to see the end of the things of this world. Somebody, probably old Nabbaye, in whose cottage he lived, always scoured him with soft soap before he started on his voyage, and in consequence a most preternatural shine overspread his blank forehead. His under jaw had a disagreeably suggestive habit of dropping, he was so feeble and so old, poor wretch !

Yet would he brighten with a faint attempt at a smile when bread and meat were put into his hands, and say, over and over again, "Ye're a Christian, ma'am; thank ye, ma'am, thank ye," thrust all that was given him, no matter what, between his one upper garment — a checked shirt — and his bare skin, and then, by way of expressing his gratitude, would strike up a dolorous quaver of—

> " Over the water and over the lea
> And over the water to Charlie,"

in a voice as querulous as a Scotch bagpipe.

Old Nabbaye, and Bennaye, her husband, with whom Peter lived, were a queer old couple. Nabbaye had a stubbly and unequal growth of sparse gray hair upon her chin, which gave her a most grim and terrible aspect, as I remember her, with the grizzled locks standing out about her head like one of the Furies. Yet she was a good enough old woman, kind to Peter and Bennaye, and kept her bit of a cottage tidy as might be. I well remember the grit of the shining sand on her scoured floor beneath my childish footsteps. The family climbed at night by a ladder up into a loft, which their little flock of fowls shared with them, to sleep. Going by the house one evening, some one heard Nabbaye call aloud to Bennaye up aloft,

"Come, Bennaye, fetch me down them heens' aigs!" To which Bennaye made answer, "I can't find no aigs! I 've looked een the bed and een under the bed, and I can't find no aigs!"

Till Bennaye grew very feeble, every summer night he paddled abroad in his dory to fish for hake, and lonely he looked, tossing among the waves, when our boat bore down and passed him with a hail which he faintly returned, as we plunged lightly through the track of the moonlight, young and happy, rejoicing in the beauty of the night, while poor Bennaye only counted his gains in the grisly hake he caught, nor considered the rubies the lighthouse scattered on the waves, or how the moon sprinkled down silver before him. He did not mind the touch of the balmy wind that blew across his weather-beaten face with the same sweet greeting that so gladdened us, but fished and fished, watching his line through the short summer night, and, when a blush of dawn stole up in the east among the stars, wound up his tackle, took his oars, and paddled home to Nabbaye with his booty, — his "fare of fish" as the natives have it. Hake-fishing after this picturesque and tedious fashion is done away with now; the islands are girdled with trawls, which catch more fish in one night than could be obtained in a week's hard labor by hand.

When the dust of Bennaye and Nabbaye was mingled in the thin earth that scarce can cover the multitude of the dead on Star Island, a youthful couple, in whom I took great interest, occupied their little house. The woman was remarkably handsome, with a beautiful head and masses of rich black hair, a face regular as the face of a Greek statue, with eyes that sparkled and cheeks that glowed, — a beauty she soon exchanged for haggard and hollow looks. As their children were born they asked my advice on the christening of each, and, being youthful and romantic, I suggested Frederick as a sounding title for the first-born boy. Taylor being the reigning President, his name was instantly added, and the child was always addressed by his whole name. Going by the house one day, my ears were assailed by a sharp outcry: "Frederick Taylor, if you don't come into the house this minute, I'll slat your head off!" The tender mother borrowed her expression from the fishermen, who disengage mackerel and other delicate-gilled fish by "slatting" them off the hook.

All this family have gone, and the house in which they lived has fallen to ruin; only the cellar remains, just such a rude hollow as those scattered over Appledore.

The people along the coast rather look down upon the Shoalers as being beyond the bounds of civilization.   A young islander was expressing his opinion on some matter to a native of Rye, who answered him with great scorn : "You don't know nothin' about it ! What do *you* know? *You* never see an apple-tree all blowed out."   A Shoaler, walking with some friends along a road in Rye, excited inextinguishable laughter by clutching his companion's sleeve as a toad hopped innocently across the way, and crying : "Mr. Berraye, what kind of a bug do you call that? D—d if I ever see such a bug as that, Mr. Berraye !" in a comical terror.   There are neither frogs nor toads at the Shoals.   "Set right down and help yourselves," said an old fellow at whose door some guests from the Shoals appeared at dinner-time. "Eat all you can.   I ain't got no manners; the girl 's got the manners, and she ain't to hum."

One old Shoaler, long since gone to another world, was a laughable and curious character. A man more wonderfully fulfilling the word "homely " in the Yankee sense, I never saw.   He had the largest, most misshapen cheek-bones ever constructed, an illimitable upper lip, teeth that should not be mentioned, and small, watery eyes. Skin and hair and eyes and mouth were of the same pasty yellow, and that grotesque head was set on a little, thin, and shambling body. He used to be head singer at the church, and "pitched the tune" by whistling when the parson had read the hymn. Then all who could joined in the singing, which must have been remarkable, to say the least. So great a power of brag is seldom found in one human being as that which permeated him from top to toe, and found vent in stories of personal prowess and bravery unexampled in history. He used to tell a story of his encounter with thirteen "Spanish grandeers" in New Orleans, he having been a sailor a great part of his life. He was innocently peering into a theatre, when the "grandeers" fell upon him out of the exceeding pride of their hearts. "Wall, sir, I turned, and I laid six o' them grandeers to the right and seven to the left, and then I put her for the old brig, and I heerd no more on 'em!"

He considered himself unequalled as a musician, and would sing you ballad after ballad, sitting bent forward with his arms on his knees, and his wrinkled eyelids screwed tight together, grinding out the tune with a quiet steadiness of purpose that seemed to betoken no end to his capacities. Ballads of love and of war he sang, — the exploits of "Brave Wolf," or, as he pronounced it, "Brahn Wolf," and one famous song of a naval battle, of which only two lines remain in my memory : —

> " With sixteen brass nineteens the Lion did growl,
>   With nineteen brass twenties the Tiger did howl."

At the close of each verse he invariably dropped his voice, and said, instead of sung, the last word, which had a most abrupt and surprising effect, to which a listener never could become accustomed. The immortal ballad of Lord Bateman he had remodelled with beautiful variations of his own. The name of the coy maiden, the Turk's only daughter, Sophia, was Susan Fryan, according to his version, and Lord Bateman was metamorphosed into Lord Bakum. When Susan Fryan crosses the sea to Lord Bakum's castle and knocks so loud that the gates do ring, he makes the bold young porter, who was so ready for to let her in, go to his master, who sits feasting with a new bride, and say : —

> " Seven long years have I tended your gate, sir,
>   Seven long years out of twenty-three,
>   But so fair a creetur as now stands waitin'
>   Never before with my eyes did see.

> " O, she has rings on every finger,
>   And round her middle if she' s one she has three ;
>   O, I 'm sure she's got more good gold about her
>   Than would buy your bride and her companie ! "

The enjoyment with which he gave this song was delightful to witness. Of the many he used to sing, one was a doleful story of how a youth of high degree fell in love with his mother's fair waiting-woman, Betsy, who was in consequence immediately transported to foreign lands. But alas for her lover! —

> " Then he fell sick and like to have died;
> His mother round his sick-bed cried,
> But all her crying it was in vain,
> For Betsy was a-ploughing the raging main! "

The word "main" was brought out with startling effect. Another song about a miller and his sons I only half remember : —

> " The miller he called his oldest son,
> Saying, ' Now my glass it is almost run,
> If I to you the mill relate,
> What toll do you *re*sign to take ? '
>
> " The son replied : ' My name is Jack,
> And out of a bushel I 'll take a peck.'
> ' Go, go, you fool! ' the old man cried,
> And called the next to his bedside.
>
> " The second said : ' My name is Ralph,
> And out of a bushel I 'll take a half.'
> ' Go, go, you fool! ' the old man cried,
> And called the next to his bedside.
>
> " The youngest said : " My name is Paul,
> And out of a bushel I 'll take it all! '
> ' You are my son ! ' the old man cried,
> And *shot* up his eyes and died in peace."

4*   F

The manner in which this last verse was delivered
was inimitable, the "died in peace" being spoken
with great satisfaction. The singer had an ancient
violin, which he used to hug under his wizened
chin, and from which he drew such dismal tones
as never before were heard on sea or land. He
had no more idea of playing than one of the cod-
fish he daily split and salted, yet he christened
with pride all the shrieks and wails he drew out
of the wretched instrument with various high-
sounding titles. After he had entertained his au-
dience for a while with these aimless sounds, he
was wont to say, "Wall, now I'll give yer Prince
Esterhazy's March," and forthwith began again
precisely the same intolerable squeak.

After he died, other stars in the musical world
appeared in the horizon, but none equalled him.
They all seemed to think it necessary to shut
their eyes and squirm like nothing human during
the process of singing a song, and they "pitched
the tune" so high that no human voice ever could
hope to reach it in safety. "Tew high, Bill, tew
high," one would say to the singer, with slow
solemnity; so Bill tried again. "Tew high again,
Bill, tew high." "Wull, *you* strike it, Obed," Bill
would say in despair; and Obed would "strike,"
and hit exactly the same impossible altitude,

whereat Bill would slap his knee, and cry in glad surprise, " D—d if he ain't got it ! " and forthwith catch Obed and launch on his perilous flight, and grow red in the face with the mighty effort of getting up there, and remaining there through the intricacies and variations of the melody. One could but wonder whence these queer tunes came, — how they were created ; some of them reminded one of the creaking and groaning of windlasses and masts, the rattling of rowlocks, the whistling of winds among cordage, yet with less of music in them than these natural sounds. The songs of the sailors heaving up the anchor are really beautiful often, the wild chant that rises sometimes into a grand chorus, all the strong voices borne out on the wind in the cry of

" Yo ho, the roaring river ! "

But these Shoals performances are lacking in any charm, except that of the broadest fun.

The process of dunning, which made the Shoals fish so famous a century ago, is almost a lost art, though the chief fisherman at Star still " duns " a few yearly. A real dunfish is handsome, cut in transparent strips, the color of brown sherry wine. The process is a tedious one : the fish are piled in the storehouse and undergo a period of "sweating" after the first drying, then are carried out into sun and wind, dried again slightly, and again piled in the warehouse, and so on till the process is complete. Drying fish in the common fashion is more difficult than might be imagined : it is necessary to watch and tend them continually as they lie on the picturesque "flakes," and if they are exposed at too early a stage to a sun too hot they burn as surely as a loaf of bread in an intemperate oven, only the burning does not crisp, but liquefies their substance.

For the last ten years fish have been caught about the Shoals by trawl and seine in such quantities that they are thinning fast, and the trade bids fair to be much less lucrative before many years have elapsed. The process of drawing the trawl is very picturesque and interesting, watched from the rocks or from the boat itself. The buoy being drawn in, then follow the baited hooks one after another. First, perhaps, a rockling shows his bright head above water ; a pull, and in he comes flapping, with brilliant red fins distended, gaping mouth, indigo-colored eyes, and richly mottled skin : a few futile somersets, and he subsides into slimy dejection. Next, perhaps, a big whelk is tossed into the boat ; then a leaden-gray haddock, with its dark stripe of color on each side ;

then, perhaps, follow a few bare hooks; then a hake, with horrid, cavernous mouth; then a large purple star-fish, or a clattering crab; then a ling, — a yellow-brown, wide-mouthed piece of ugliness never eaten here, but highly esteemed on the coast of Scotland; then more cod or haddock, or perhaps a lobster, bristling with indignation at the novel situation in which he finds himself; then a cusk, long, smooth, compact, and dark; then a catfish. Of all fiends commend me to the catfish as the most fiendish! Black as night, with thick and hideous skin, which looks a dull, mouldy green beneath the water, a head shaped as much like a cat's as a fish's head can be, in which the devil's own eyes seem to glow with a dull, malicious gleam, — and such a mouth! What terrible expressions these cold creatures carry to and fro in the vast, dim spaces of the sea! All fish have a more or less imbecile and wobegone aspect; but this one looks absolutely evil, and Schiller might well say of him that he "grins through the grate of his spiky teeth," and sharp and deadly are they; every man looks out for his boots when a catfish comes tumbling in, for they bite through leather, flesh, and bones. They seize a ballast-stone between their jaws, and their teeth snap and fly in all directions. I have seen them bite the long

blade of a sharp knife so fiercely, that, when it
was lifted and held aloft, they kept their furious
gripe, and dangled, flapping all their clumsy
weight, hanging by their teeth to the blade.
Sculpins abound, and are a nuisance on the
trawls. Ugly and grotesque as are the full-grown
fish, there is nothing among the finny tribe more
dainty, more quaint and delicate, than the baby
sculpin. Sometimes in a pool of crystal water
one comes upon him unawares, — a fairy creature,
the color of a blush-rose, striped and freaked and
pied with silver and gleaming green, hanging in
the almost invisible water as a bird in air, with
broad, transparent fins suffused with a faint pink
color, stretched wide like wings to upbear the
supple form. The curious head is only strange,
not hideous as yet, and one gazes marvelling at
all the beauty lavished on a thing of so little
worth.

Wolf-fish, first cousins to the catfish, are found
also on the trawls; and dog-fish, with pointed
snouts and sand-paper skins, abound to such an
extent as to drive away everything else sometimes.
Sand-dabs, a kind of flounder, fasten their slug-
gish bodies to the hooks, and a few beautiful red
fish, called bream, are occasionally found; also a
few blue-fish and sharks; frequently halibut, —

though these latter are generally caught on trawls
which are made especially for them. Sometimes
is caught on a trawl a monstrous creature of horrible aspect, called the nurse-fish, — an immense
fish weighing twelve hundred pounds, with a
skin like a nutmeg-grater, and no teeth, — a kind
of sucker, hence its name. I asked a Shoaler
what the nurse-fish looked like, and he answered
promptly, "Like the Devil!" One weighing
twelve hundred pounds has "two barrels of
liver," as the natives phrase it, which is very
valuable for the oil it contains. One of the fishermen described a creature which they call mud-
eel, — a foot and a half long, with a mouth like a
rat, and two teeth. The bite of this water-snake
is poisonous, the islanders aver, and tell a story
of a man bitten by one at Mount Desert last
year, "who did not live long enough to get to the
doctor." They bite at the hooks on the trawl, and
are drawn up in a lump of mud, and the men cut
the ropes and mangle their lines to get rid of
them. Huge sunfish are sometimes harpooned,
lying on the top of the water, — a lump of flesh
like cocoanut meat encased in a skin like rubber
cloth, with a most dim and abject hint of a face,
absurdly disproportionate to the size of the body,
roughly outlined on the edge. Sword-fish are

also harpooned, weighing eight hundred pounds and upward; they are very delicate food. A sword-fish swimming leaves a wake a mile long on a calm day, and bewilders the imagination into a belief in sea-serpents. There's a legend that a torpedo was caught here once upon a time; and the thrasher, fox-shark, or sea-fox occasionally alarms the fisherman with his tremendous flexible tail, that reaches "from the gunnel to the mainmast-top" when the creature comes to the surface. Also they tell of skip-jacks that sprang on board their boats at night when they were hake-fishing, — "little things about as large as mice, long and slender, with beaks like birds." Sometimes a huge horse-mackerel flounders in and drives ashore on a ledge, for the gulls to scream over for weeks. Mackerel, herring, porgies, and shiners used to abound before the seines so thinned them. Bonito and blue-fish and dog-fish help drive away the more valuable varieties. It is a lovely sight to see a herring-net drawn in, especially by moonlight, when every fish hangs like a long silver drop from the close-set meshes. Perch are found in inexhaustible quantities about the rocks, and lump or butter fish are sometimes caught; pollock are very plentiful, — smooth, graceful, slender creatures! It is fascinating to

watch them turning somersets in the water close
to the shore in full tides, or following a boat at
sunset, and breaking the molten gold of the sea's
surface with silver-sparkling fin and tail. The
rudder-fish is sometimes found, and alewives and
menhaden. Whales are more or less plentiful in
summer, " spouting their foam-fountains in the
sea." Beautiful is the sparkling column of water
rising suddenly afar off and falling noiselessly
back again. Not long ago a whale twisted his
tail in the cable of the schooner Vesper, lying
to the eastward of the Shoals, and towed the vessel several miles, at the rate of twenty knots an
hour, with the water boiling all over her from
stem to stern !

Last winter some of the Shoalers were drawing
a trawl between the Shoals and Boone Island,
fifteen miles to the eastward. As they drew in
the line and relieved each hook of its burden, lo !
a horror was lifted half above the surface, — part
of a human body, which dropped off the hooks
and was gone, while they shuddered, and stared at
each other, aghast at the hideous sight.

Porpoises are seen at all seasons. I never saw
one near enough to gain a knowledge of its expression, but it always seemed to me that these
fish led a more hilarious life than the greater part

of their race, and I think they must carry less
dejected countenances than most of the inhabitants of the sea.   They frisk so delightfully on
the surface, and ponderously plunge over and over
with such apparent gayety and satisfaction!   I
remember being out one moonless summer night
beyond the lighthouse island, in a little boat filled
with gay young people.   The sea was like oil, the
air was thick and warm, no star broke the upper
darkness, only now and then the lighthouse threw
its jewelled track along the water, and through
the dense air its long rays stretched above, turning solemnly, like the luminous spokes of a gigantic
wheel, as the lamps slowly revolved.   There had
been much talk and song and laughter, much playing with the warm waves (or rather smooth undulations of the sea, for there was n't a breath of
wind to make a ripple), which broke at a touch
into pale-green, phosphorescent fire.   Beautiful
arms, made bare to the shoulder, thrust down into
the liquid darkness, shone flaming silver and gold;
from the fingers playing beneath, fire seemed to
stream; emerald sparks clung to the damp draperies; and a splashing oar-blade half revealed
sweet faces and bright young eyes.   Suddenly a
pause came in talk and song and laughter, and in
the unaccustomed silence we seemed to be waiting

for something. At once out of the darkness came a slow, tremendous sigh that made us shiver in the soft air, as if all the woe and terror of the sea were condensed in that immense and awful breath ; and we took our oars and pulled homeward, with the weird fires flashing from our bows and oar-blades. " Only a porpoise blowing," said the initiated, when we told our tale. It may have been " only a porpoise blowing "; but the leviathan himself could hardly have made a more prodigious sound.

Within the lovely limits of summer it is beautiful to live almost anywhere ; most beautiful where the ocean meets the land ; and here particularly, where all the varying splendor of the sea encompasses the place, and the ceaseless changing of the tides brings continual refreshment into the life of every day. But summer is late and slow to come ; and long after the mainland has begun to bloom and smile beneath the influence of spring, the bitter northwest winds still sweep the cold, green water about these rocks, and tear its surface into long and glittering waves from morning till night, and from night till morning, through many weeks. No leaf breaks the frozen soil, and no bud swells on the shaggy bushes that clothe the slopes. But if summer is a laggard in her coming, she makes up for it by the loveliness of her lingering into autumn; for when the pride of trees and flowers is despoiled by frost on shore, the little gardens here are glowing at their brightest, and day after day of mellow splendor drops like a benediction from the hand of God. In the early mornings in September the mists draw away from the depths of inland valleys, and rise into the lucid western sky, — tall columns and towers of cloud, solid, compact, superb; their pure, white, shining heads uplifted into the ether, solemn, stately, and still, till some wandering breeze disturbs their perfect outline, and they melt about the heavens in scattered fragments as the day goes on. Then there are mornings when "all in the blue, unclouded weather" the coast-line comes out so distinctly that houses, trees, bits of white beach, are clearly visible, and with a glass, moving forms of carriages and cattle are distinguishable nine miles away. In the transparent air the peaks of Mounts Madison, Washington, and Jefferson are seen distinctly at a distance of one hundred miles. In the early light even the green color of the trees is perceptible on the Rye shore. All through these quiet days the air is full of wandering thistle-down, the inland golden-rod

waves its plumes, and close by the water's edge,
in rocky clefts, its seaside sister blossoms in
gorgeous color ; the rose-haws redden, the iris
unlocks its shining caskets, and casts its closely
packed seeds about, gray berries cluster on the
bayberry-bushes, the sweet life-everlasting sends
out its wonderful, delicious fragrance, and the pale
asters spread their flowers in many-tinted sprays.
Through October and into November the fair,
mild weather lasts. At the first breath of October, the hillside at Appledore fires up with the
living crimson of the huckleberry-bushes, as if a
blazing torch had been applied to it ; the slanting
light at sunrise and sunset makes a wonderful glory
across it. The sky deepens its blue ; beneath it
the brilliant sea glows into violet, and flashes into
splendid purple where the " tide-rip," or eddying
winds, make long streaks across its surface (poets
are not wrong who talk of "purple seas,") the
air is clear and sparkling, the lovely summer haze
withdraws, all things take a crisp and tender
outline, and the cry of the curlew and the plover
is doubly sweet through the pure, cool air. Then
sunsets burn in clear and tranquil skies, or flame
in piled magnificence of clouds. Some night a
long bar lies, like a smouldering brand, along the
horizon, deep carmine where the sun has touched

it ; and out of that bar breaks a sudden gale before morning, and a fine fury and tumult begins to rage. Then comes the fitful weather, — wild winds and hurrying waves, low, scudding clouds, tremendous rains that shut out everything ; and the rocks lie weltering between the sea and sky, with the brief fire of the leaves quenched and swept away on the hillside, — only rushing wind and streaming water everywhere, as if a second deluge were flooding the world.

After such a rain comes a gale from the southeast to sweep the sky clear, — a gale so furious that it blows the sails straight out of the bolt-ropes, if any vessel is so unfortunate as to be caught in it with a rag of canvas aloft ; and the coast is strewn with the wrecks of such craft as happen to be caught on the lee shore, for

" Anchors drag, and topmasts lap,"

and nothing can hold against this terrible, blind fury. It is appalling to listen to the shriek of such a wind, even though one is safe upon a rock that cannot move ; and more dreadful is it to see the destruction one cannot lift a finger to avert.

As the air grows colder, curious atmospheric effects become visible. At the first biting cold the distant mainland has the appearance of being taken off its feet, as it were, — the line shrunken and

distorted, detached from the water at both ends :
it is as if one looked under it and saw the sky beyond. Then, on bright mornings with a brisk wind,
little wafts of mist rise between the quick, short
waves, and melt away before noon. At some periods of intense cold these mists, which are never in
banks like fog, rise in irregular, whirling columns
reaching to the clouds, — shadowy phantoms, torn
and wild, that stalk past like Ossian's ghosts, solemnly and noiselessly throughout the bitter day.
When the sun drops down behind these weird
processions, with a dark-red, lurid light, it is like a
vast conflagration, wonderful and terrible to see.
The columns, that strike and fall athwart the
island, sweep against the windows with a sound
like sand, and lie on the ground in ridges, like fine,
sharp hail; yet the heavens are clear, the heavily
rolling sea dark-green and white, and, between the
breaking crests, the misty columns stream toward
the sky.

Sometimes a totally different vapor, like cold,
black smoke, rolls out from the land, and flows
over the sea to an unknown distance, swallowing
up the islands on its way. Its approach is hideous
to witness. "It 's all thick o' black vapor," some
islander announces, coming in from out of doors;
just as they say, "It 's all thick o' white foam,"

when the sudden squall tears the sea into fringes of spray.

In December the colors seem to fade out of the world, and utter ungraciousness prevails. The great, cool, whispering, delicious sea, that encircled us with a thousand caresses the beautiful summer through, turns slowly our sullen and inveterate enemy; leaden it lies beneath a sky like tin, and rolls its " white, cold, heavy-plunging foam" against a shore of iron. Each island wears its chalk-white girdle of ice between the rising and falling tides (edged with black at low-water, where the lowest-growing seaweed is exposed), making the stern bare rocks above more forbidding by their contrast with its stark whiteness, — and the whiteness of salt-water ice is ghastly. Nothing stirs abroad, except perhaps

> " A lonely sea-bird crosses,
>   With one waft of wing,"

your view, as you gaze from some spray-incrusted window; or you behold the weather-beaten schooners creeping along the blurred coast-line from Cape Elizabeth and the northern ports of Maine towards Cape Ann, laden with lumber or lime, and sometimes, rarely, with hay or provisions.

After winter has fairly set in, the lonely dwellers

at the Isles of Shoals find life quite as much as
they can manage, being so entirely thrown upon
their own resources that it requires all the philos-
ophy at their disposal to answer the demand. In
the village, where several families make a little
community, there should be various human interests outside each separate fireside ; but of their
mode of life I know little. Upon three of the
islands live isolated families, cut off by the " always wind-obeying deep" from each other and
from the mainland, sometimes for weeks together,
when the gales are fiercest, with no letters nor
intercourse with any living thing. Some sullen
day in December the snow begins to fall, and the
last touch of desolation is laid upon the scene ;
there is nothing any more but white snow and
dark water, hemmed in by a murky horizon ; and
nothing moves or sounds within its circle but the
sea harshly assailing the shore, and the chill wind
that sweeps across. Toward night the wind begins to rise, the snow whirls and drifts, and clings
wherever it can find a resting-place ; and though
so much is blown away, yet there is enough left to
smother up the rock and make it almost impossible to move about on it. The drifts sometimes
are very deep in the hollows ; one winter, sixteen
sheep were buried in a drift, in which they re-

5   G

mained a week, and, strange to say, only one was
dead when they were discovered. One goes to
sleep in the muffled roar of the storm, and wakes
to find it still raging with senseless fury; all day
it continues; towards night the curtain of falling
flakes withdraws, a faint light shows westward;
slowly the clouds roll together, the lift grows bright
with pale, clear blue over the land, the wind has
hauled to the northwest, and the storm is at an
end. When the clouds are swept away by the
besom of the pitiless northwest, how the stars
glitter in the frosty sky! What wondrous streamers of northern lights flare through the winter
darkness! I have seen the sky at midnight crimson and emerald and orange and blue in palpitat-
ing sheets along the whole northern half of the
heavens, or rosy to the zenith, or belted with a
bar of solid yellow light from east to west, as if
the world were a basket, and it the golden handle
thereto. The weather becomes of the first importance to the dwellers on the rock; the changes of
the sky and sea, the flitting of the coasters to and
fro, the visits of the sea-fowl, sunrise and sunset,
the changing moon, the northern lights, the constellations that wheel in splendor through the
winter night, — all are noted with a love and
careful scrutiny that is seldom given by people

living in populous places.   One grows accustomed
to the aspect of the constellations, and they seem
like the faces of old friends looking down out of
the awful blackness; and when in summer the
great Orion disappears, how it is missed out of
the sky!   I remember the delight with which we
caught a glimpse of the planet Mercury, in March,
1868, following close at the heels of the sinking
sun, redly shining in the reddened horizon, — a
stranger mysterious and utterly unknown before.

For these things make our world : there are no
lectures, operas, concerts, theatres, no music of
any kind, except what the waves may whisper in
rarely gentle moods ; no galleries of wonders like
the Natural History rooms, in which it is so fascinating to wander; no streets, shops, carriages,
no postman, no neighbors, not a door-bell within
the compass of the place!   Never was life so ex-
empt from interruptions.   The eight or ten small
schooners that carry on winter fishing, flying to
and fro through foam and squall to set and haul
in their trawls, at rare intervals bring a mail, —
an accumulation of letters, magazines, and newspapers that it requires a long time to plod through.
This is the greatest excitement of the long winters ; and no one can truly appreciate the delight
of letters till he has lived where he can hear from
his friends only once in a month.

But the best balanced human mind is prone to lose its elasticity, and stagnate, in this isolation. One learns immediately the value of work to keep one's wits clear, cheerful, and steady ; just as much real work of the body as it can bear without weariness being always beneficent, but here indispensable.   And in this matter women have the advantage of men, who are condemned to fold their hands when their tasks are done.   No woman need ever have a vacant minute, — there are so many pleasant, useful things which she may, and had better do.   Blessed be the man who invented knitting !   (I never heard that a woman invented this or any other art.)   It is the most charming and picturesque of quiet occupations, leaving the knitter free to read aloud, or talk, or think, while steadily and surely beneath the flying fingers the comfortable stocking grows.

No one can dream what a charm there is in taking care of pets, singing-birds, plants, etc., with such advantages of solitude ; how every leaf and bud and flower is pored over, and admired, and loved !   A whole conservatory, flushed with azaleas, and brilliant with forests of camellias and every precious exotic that blooms, could not impart so much delight as I have known a single rose to give, unfolding in the bleak bitterness of a day

in February, when this side of the planet seemed
to have arrived at its culmination of hopelessness,
with the Isles of Shoals the most hopeless speck
upon its surface.   One gets close to the heart of
these things ; they are almost as precious as Pic-
ciola to the prisoner, and yield a fresh and constant joy, such as the pleasure-seeking inhabitants
of cities could not find in their whole round of
shifting diversions.   With a bright and cheerful
interior, open fires, books, and pictures, windows
full of thrifty blossoming plants and climbing vines,
a family of singing-birds, plenty of work, and a
clear head and quiet conscience, it would go hard
if. one could not be happy even in such loneliness.
Books, of course, are inestimable.   Nowhere does
one follow a play of Shakespeare's with greater
zest, for it brings the whole world, which you need,
about you ; doubly precious the deep thoughts
wise men have given to help us, — doubly sweet
the songs of all the poets ; for nothing comes between to distract you.

One realizes how hard it was for Robinson Cru-
soe to keep the record of his lonely days ; for
even in a family of eight or nine the succession is
kept with difficulty.   I recollect that, after an
unusually busy Saturday, when household work
was done, and lessons said, and the family were

looking forward to Sunday and merited leisure, at sunset came a young Star-Islander on some errand to our door. One said to him, "Well, Jud, how many fish have they caught to-day at Star?" Jud looked askance and answered, like one who did not wish to be trifled with, "We don't go a-fishing Sundays!" So we had lost our Sunday, thinking it was Saturday; and next day began the usual business, with no break of refreshing rest between.

Though the thermometer says that here it is twelve degrees warmer in winter than on the main-land, the difference is hardly perceptible, — the situation is so bleak, while the winds of the north and west bite like demons, with all the bitter breath of the snowy continent condensed in their deadly chill. Easterly and southerly gales are milder; we have no east winds such as sadden humanity on shore; they are tempered to gentle-ness by some mysterious means. Sometimes there are periods of cold which, though not intense (the mercury seldom falling lower than 11° above zero), are of such long duration that the fish are killed in the sea. This happens frequently with perch, the dead bodies of which strew the shores and float on the water in masses. Sometimes ice forms in the mouth of the Piscataqua River, which, contin-

ually broken into unequal blocks by the rushing
tide and the immense pressure of the outer ocean,
fills the space between the islands and the shore,
so that it is very difficult to force a boat through.
The few schooners moored about the islands become so loaded with ice that sometimes they sink ;
every plunge into the assailing waves adds a fresh
crust, infinitely thin ; but in twenty-four hours
enough accumulates to sink the vessel ; and it is
part of the day's work in the coldest weather to
beat off the ice, — and hard work it is. Every
time the bowsprit dips under, the man who sits
astride it is immersed to his waist in the freezing
water, as he beats at the bow to free the laboring
craft. I cannot imagine a harder life than the
sailors lead in winter in the coasting-vessels that
stream in endless processions to and fro along the
shore ; and they seem to be the hardest set of
people under the sun, — so rough and reckless that
they are not pleasant even at a distance. Sometimes they land here. A crew of thirteen or fourteen came on shore last winter ; they might
have been the ghosts of the men who manned the
picaroons that used to swarm in these seas. A
more piratical-looking set could not well be imagined. They roamed about, and glared in at the
windows with weather-beaten, brutal faces, and

eyes that showed traces of whiskey, ugly and un-
mistakable.

No other visitors break the solitude of Appledore, except neighbors from Star once in a while;
if any one is sick, they send, perhaps, for medicine
or milk; or they bring some rare fish; or if any
one dies, and they cannot reach the mainland,
they come to get a coffin made. I never shall forget one long, dreary, drizzly northeast storm, when
two men rowed across from Star to Appledore on
this errand. A little child had died, and they
could not sail to the mainland, and had no means
to construct a coffin among themselves. All day
I watched the making of that little chrysalis; and
at night the last nail was driven in, and it lay
across a bench in the midst of the litter of the
workshop, and a curious stillness seemed to ema-
nate from the senseless boards. I went back to
the house and gathered a handful of scarlet gera-
nium, and returned with it through the rain.
The brilliant blossoms were sprinkled with glittering drops. I laid them in the little coffin, while
the wind wailed so sorrowfully outside, and the
rain poured against the windows. Two men came
through the mist and storm, and one swung the
light little shell to his shoulder, and they carried
it away, and the gathering darkness shut down and

hid them as they tossed among the waves. I never saw the little girl, but where they buried her I know: the lighthouse shines close by, and every night the quiet, constant ray steals to her grave and softly touches it, as if to say, with a caress, "Sleep well! Be thankful you are spared so much that I see humanity endure, fixed here forever where I stand!"

It is exhilarating, spite of the intense cold, to wake to the brightness the northwest gale always brings, after the hopeless smother of a prolonged snow-storm. The sea is deep indigo, whitened with flashing waves all over the surface; the sky is speckless; no cloud passes across it the whole day long; and the sun sets red and clear, without any abatement of the wind. The spray flying on the western shore for a moment is rosy as the sinking sun shines through, but for a moment only, — and again there is nothing but the ghastly whiteness of the salt-water ice, the cold, gray rock, the sullen, foaming brine, the unrelenting heavens, and the sharp wind cutting like a knife. All night long it roars beneath the hollow sky, — roars still at sunrise. Again the day passes precisely like the one gone before; the sun lies in a glare of quicksilver on the western water, sinks again in the red west to rise on just such another day;

5

and thus goes on, for weeks sometimes, with an exasperating pertinacity that would try the most philosophical patience.   There comes a time when just that glare of quicksilver on the water is not to be endured a minute longer.   During this period no boat goes to or comes from the mainland, and the prisoners on the rock are cut off from all intercourse with their kind.   Abroad, only the cattle move, crowding into the sunniest corners, and stupidly chewing the cud ; and the hens and ducks, that chatter and cackle and cheerfully crow in spite of fate and the northwest gale.   The dauntless and graceful gulls soar on their strong pinions over the drift cast up about the coves. Sometimes flocks of snow-buntings wheel about the house and pierce the loud breathing of the wind with sweet, wild cries.   And often the spectral arctic owl may be seen on a height, sitting upright, like a column of snow, its large, round head slowly turning from left to right, ever on the alert, watching for the rats that plague the settlement almost as grievously as they did Hamelin town, in Brunswick, five hundred years ago.'

How the rats came here first is not known ; probably some old ship imported them.   They live partly on mussels, the shells of which lie in heaps about their holes, as the violet-lined fresh-

water shells lie about the nests of the muskrats
on the mainland.   They burrow among the rocks
close to the shore, in favorable spots, and, somewhat like the moles, make subterranean galleries,
whence they issue at low tide, and, stealing to the
crevices of seaweed-curtained rocks, they fall upon
and dislodge any unfortunate crabs they may find,
and kill and devour them.   Many a rat has caught
a Tartar in this perilous kind of hunting, has been
dragged into the sea and killed, — drowned in the
clutches of the crab he sought to devour ; for the
strength of these shell-fish is something astonish-
ing.

Several snowy owls haunt the islands the whole
winter long.   I have never heard them cry like
other owls ; when disturbed or angry, they make
a sound like a watchman's rattle, very loud and
harsh, or they whistle with intense shrillness, like
a human being.   Their habitual silence adds to
their ghostliness ; and when at noonday they sit,
high up, snow-white above the snow-drifts, blink-
ing their pale yellow eyes in the sun, they are
weird indeed.   One night in March I saw one
perched upon a rock between me and the "last
remains of sunset dimly burning " in the west, his
curious outline drawn black against the redness of
the sky, his large head bent forward, and the

whole aspect meditative and most human in its
expression.   I longed to go out and sit beside him
and talk to him in the twilight, to ask of him the
story of his life, or, if he would have permitted it,
to watch him without a word.   The plumage of
this creature is wonderfully beautiful, — white,
with scattered spots like little flecks of tawny
cloud, — and his black beak and talons are powerful and sharp as iron ; he might literally grapple
his friend, or his enemy, with hooks of steel.   As
he is clothed in a mass of down, his outlines are
so soft that he is like an enormous snowflake while
flying ; and he is a sight worth seeing when he
stretches wide his broad wings, and sweeps down
on his prey, silent and swift, with an unerring aim,
and bears it off to the highest rock he can find,
to devour it.   In the summer one finds frequently
upon the heights a little, solid ball of silvery fur
and pure white bones, washed and bleached by
the rain and sun ; it is the rat's skin and skeleton
in a compact bundle, which the owl rejects after
having swallowed it.

Some quieter day, on the edge of a southerly
wind, perhaps, boats go out over the gray, sad
water after sea-fowl, — the murres that swim in
little companies, keeping just out of reach of
shot, and are so spiteful that they beat the boat

with their beaks, when wounded, in impotent
rage, till they are despatched with an oar or
another shot ; or kittiwakes, — exquisite creatures
like living forms of snow and cloud in color, with
beaks and feet of dull gold, — that come when
you wave a white handkerchief, and flutter almost
within reach of your hand; or oldwives, called by
the natives *scoldenores*, with clean white caps ; or
clumsy eider-ducks, or coots, or mergansers, or
whatever they may find.   Black ducks, of course,
are often shot.   Their jet-black, shining plumage
is splendidly handsome, set off with the broad,
flame-colored beak.   Little auks, stormy-petrels,
loons, grebes, lords-and-ladies, sea-pigeons, sea-
parrots, various guillemots, and all sorts of gulls
abound.   Sometimes an eagle sweeps over ; gan-
nets pay occasional visits ; the great blue heron is
often seen in autumn and spring.   One of the
most striking birds is the cormorant, called here
" shag " ; from it the rock at Duck Island takes its
name.   It used to be an object of almost awful
interest to me when I beheld it perched upon
White Island Head, — a solemn figure, high and
dark against the clouds.   Once, while living on
that island, in the thickest of a great storm in
autumn, when we seemed to be set between two
contending armies, deafened by the continuous

cannonading of breakers, and lashed and beaten by winds and waters till it was almost impossible to hear ourselves speak, we became aware of another sound, which pierced to our ears, bringing a sudden terror lest it should be the voices of human beings. Opening the window a little, what a wild combination of sounds came shrieking in! A large flock of wild geese had settled for safety upon the rock, and completely surrounded us, — agitated, clamorous, weary. We might have secured any number of them, but it would have been a shameful thing. We were glad, indeed, that they should share our little foothold in that chaos, and they flew away unhurt when the tempest lulled. I was a very young child when this happened, but I never can forget that autumn night, — it seemed so wonderful and pitiful that those storm-beaten birds should have come crying to our rock; and the strange, wild chorus that swept in when the window was pried open a little took so strong a hold upon my imagination that I shall hear it as long as I live. The lighthouse, so beneficent to mankind, is the destroyer of birds, — of land birds particularly, though in thick weather sea-birds are occasionally bewildered into breaking their heads against the glass, plunging forward headlong towards the light, just as the frail moth of summer evenings madly seeks its death in the candle's blaze. Sometimes in autumn, always in spring, when birds are migrating, they are destroyed in such quantities by this means that it is painful to reflect upon. The keeper living at the island three years ago told me that he picked up three hundred and seventy-five in one morning at the foot of the lighthouse, all dead. They fly with such force against the glass that their beaks are often splintered. The keeper said he found the destruction greatest in hazy weather, and he thought "they struck a ray at a great distance and followed it up." Many a May morning have I wandered about the rock at the foot of the tower mourning over a little apron brimful of sparrows, swallows, thrushes, robins, fire-winged blackbirds, many-colored warblers and fly-catchers, beautifully clothed yellow-birds, nuthatches, cat-birds, even the purple finch and scarlet tanager and golden oriole, and many more beside, — enough to break the heart of a small child to think of! Once a great eagle flew against the lantern and shivered the glass. That was before I lived there; but after we came, two gulls cracked one of the large, clear panes, one stormy night.

The sea-birds are comparatively few and shy at

this time; but I remember when they were plentiful enough, when on Duck Island in summer the
"medrakes," or tern, made rude nests on the
beach, and the little yellow gulls, just out of the
eggs, ran tumbling about among the stones, hiding their foolish heads in every crack and cranny,
and, like the ostrich, imagining themselves safe so
long as they could not see the danger.   And even
now the sandpipers build in numbers on the
islands, and the young birds, which look like tiny
tufts of fog, run about among the bayberry-
bushes, with sweet, scared piping.   They are ex-
quisitely beautiful and delicate, covered with a
down just like gray mist, with brilliant black eyes,
and slender, graceful legs that make one think of
grass-stems.   And here the loons congregate in
spring and autumn.   These birds seem to me the
most human and at the same time the most de-
moniac of their kind.   I learned to imitate their
different cries; they are wonderful !   At one time
the loon language was so familiar that I could almost always summon a considerable flock by
going down to the water and assuming the neigh-
borly and conversational tone which they generally
use : after calling a few minutes, first a far-off
voice responded, then other voices answered him,
and when this was kept up a while, half a dozen

birds would come sailing in. It was the most delightful little party imaginable; so comical were they, so entertaining, that it was impossible not to laugh aloud, — and they could laugh too, in a way which chilled the marrow of one's bones. They always laugh, when shot at, if they are missed; as the Shoalers say, "They laugh like a warrior." But their long, wild, melancholy cry before a storm is the most awful note I ever heard from a bird. It is so sad, so hopeless, — a clear, high shriek, shaken, as it drops into silence, into broken notes that make you think of the fluttering of a pennon in the wind, — a shudder of sound. They invariably utter this cry before a storm.

Between the gales from all points of the compass, that

> "'twixt the green sea and the azured vault
> Set roaring war,"

some day there falls a dead calm; the whole expanse of the ocean is like a mirror; there's not a whisper of a wave, not a sigh from any wind about the world, — an awful, breathless pause prevails. Then if a loon swims into the motionless little bights about the island, and raises his weird cry, the silent rocks re-echo the unearthly tone, and it seems as if the creature were in league with the mysterious forces that are so soon to turn this

H

deathly stillness into confusion and dismay. All through the day the ominous quiet lasts; in the afternoon, while yet the sea is glassy, a curious undertone of mournful sound can be perceived, — not fitful, — a steady moan such as the wind makes over the mouth of an empty jar. Then the islanders say, "Do you hear Hog Island crying? Now look out for a storm!" No one knows how that low moaning is produced, or why Appledore, of all the islands, should alone lament before the tempest. Through its gorges, perhaps, some current of wind sighs with that hollow cry. Yet the sea could hardly keep its unruffled surface were a wind abroad sufficient to draw out the boding sound. Such a calm preceded the storm which destroyed the Minot's Ledge Lighthouse in 1849. I never knew such silence. Though the sun blazed without a cloud, the sky and sea were utterly wan and colorless, and before sunset the mysterious tone began to vibrate in the breezeless air. "Hog Island's crying!" said the islanders. One could but think of the Ancient Mariner, as the angry sun went down in a brassy glare, and still no ripple broke the calm. But with the twilight gathered the waiting wind, slowly and steadily; and before morning the shock of the breakers was like the incessant thundering of heavy guns;

the solid rock perceptibly trembled; windows shook, and glass and china rattled in the house. It is impossible to describe the confusion, the tumult, the rush and roar and thunder of waves and wind overwhelming those rocks, — the whole Atlantic rushing headlong to cast itself upon them. It was very exciting: the most timid among us lost all sense of fear. Before the next night the sea had made a breach through the valley on Appledore, in which the houses stand, — a thing that never had happened within the memory of the oldest inhabitant. The waves piled in from the eastward (where Old Harry was tossing the breakers sky-high), — a maddened troop of giants, sweeping everything before them, — and followed one another, white as milk, through the valley from east to west, strewing the space with boulders from a solid wall six feet high and as many thick, which ran across the top of the beach, and which one tremendous wave toppled over like a child's fence of blocks. Kelp and sea-weed were piled in banks high up along the shore, and strewed the doorsteps; and thousands of the hideous creatures known among the Shoalers as sea-mice, a holothurian (a livid, shapeless mass of torpid life), were scattered in all directions. While the storm was at its height, it was impossible to do anything but watch it through windows beaten by the blinding spray which burst in flying clouds all over the island, drenching every inch of the soil in foaming brine. In the coves the "yeasty surges" were churned into yellow masses of foam, that blew across in trembling flakes, and clung wherever they lit, leaving a hoary scum of salt when dry, which remained till sweet, fair water dropped out of the clouds to wash it all away. It was long before the sea went down; and, days after the sun began to shine, the fringe of spray still leaped skyward from the eastern shore, and Shag and Mingo Rocks at Duck Island tossed their distant clouds of snow against the blue.

After the wind subsided, it was curious to examine the effects of the breakers on the eastern shore, where huge masses of rock were struck off from the cliffs, and flung among the wild heaps of scattered boulders, to add to the already hopeless confusion of the gorges. The eastern aspects of the islands change somewhat every year or two from this cause; and, indeed, over all their surfaces continual change goes on from the action of the weather. Under the hammer and chisel of frost and heat, masses of stone are detached and fall from the edges of cliffs, whole ledges become disintegrated, the rock cracks in smooth, thin sheets, and, once loosened, the whole mass can be pulled out, sheet by sheet. Twenty years ago those subtle, irresistible tools of the weather had cracked off a large mass of rock from a ledge on the slope of a gentle declivity. I could just lay my hand in the space then : now three men can walk abreast between the ledge and the detached mass ; and nothing has touched it save heat and cold. The whole aspect of the rocks is infinitely aged. I never can see the beautiful salutation of sunrise upon their hoary fronts, without thinking how many millions of times they have answered to that delicate touch. On Boone Island, — a low, dangerous rock fifteen miles east of the Shoals, — the sea has even greater opportunities of destruction, the island is so low. Once, after a stormy night, the lighthouse-keeper told me the family found a great stone, weighing half a ton, in the back entry, which Father Neptune had deposited there, — his card, with his compliments !

Often tremendous breakers encompass the islands when the surface of the sea is perfectly calm and the weather serene and still, — the results of great storms far out at sea. A "long swell" swings indolently, and the ponderous waves roll in as if tired and half asleep, to burst into clouds of

splendor against the cliffs.   Very different is their
hurried, eager breaking when the shoulder of a
gale compels them.   There is no sound more
gentle, more slumberous, than the distant roll of
these billows, —

> " The rolling sea resounding soft,"

as Spenser has it.   The rush of a fully alive and
closely pursued breaker is, at a distance, precisely
like that which a rocket makes, sweeping headlong
upward through the air; but the other is a long
and peaceful sigh, a dreamy, lulling, beautiful
sound, which produces a Lethean forgetfulness of
care and pain, makes all earthly ill seem unreal,
and it is as if one wandered

> "In dreamful wastes, where footless fancies dwell."

It requires a strong effort to emerge from this
lotus-eating state of mind.   O, lovely it is, on
sunny afternoons to sit high up in a crevice of the
rock and look down on the living magnificence of
breakers such as made music about us after the
Minot's Ledge storm, — to watch them gather,
one after another,

> " Cliffs of emerald topped with snow,
>   That lift and lift, and then let go
>   A great white avalanche of thunder,"

which makes the solid earth tremble, and you,
clinging to the moist rock, feel like a little cockle-

shell! If you are out of the reach of the heavy fall of spray, the fine salt mist will still stream about you, and salute your cheek with the healthful freshness of the brine, make your hair damp, and encrust your eyebrows with salt. While you sit watching the shifting splendor, uprises at once a higher cloud than usual; and across it springs a sudden rainbow, like a beautiful thought beyond the reach of human expression. High over your head the white gulls soar, gathering the sunshine in the snowy hollows of their wings. As you look up to them floating in the fathomless blue, there is something awful in the purity of that arch beneath their wings, in light or shade, as the broad pinions move with stately grace. There is no bird so white, — nor swan, nor dove, nor mystic ibis : about the ocean-marges there is no dust to soil their perfect snow, and no stormy wind can ruffle their delicate plumes, — the beautiful, happy creatures! One never tires of watching them. Again and again appears the rainbow with lovely colors melting into each other and vanishing, to appear again at the next upspringing of the spray. On the horizon the white sails shine; and far and wide spreads the blue of the sea, with nothing between you and the eastern continent across its vast, calm plain.

I well remember my first sight of White Island, where we took up our abode on leaving the mainland. I was scarcely five years old; but from the upper windows of our dwelling in Portsmouth, I had been shown the clustered masts of ships lying at the wharves along the Piscataqua River, faintly outlined against the sky, and, baby as I was, even then I was drawn, with a vague longing, seaward. How delightful was that long, first sail to the Isles of Shoals! How pleasant the unaccustomed sound of the incessant ripple against the boat-side, the sight of the wide water and limitless sky, the warmth of the broad sunshine that made us blink like young sandpipers as we sat in triumph, perched among the household goods with which the little craft was laden! It was at sunset in autumn that we were set ashore on that loneliest, lovely rock, where the lighthouse looked down on us like some tall, black-capped giant, and filled me with awe and wonder. At its base a few goats were grouped on the rock, standing out dark against the red sky as I looked up at them. The stars were beginning to twinkle; the wind blew cold, charged with the sea's sweetness; the sound of many waters half bewildered me. Some one began to light the lamps in the tower. Rich red and golden, they swung round in mid-air; everything was strange

WHITE ISLAND.

Smuttynose buildings included, from left, the Mid-Ocean House, a hotel owned by Thomas Laighton, father of the author, the Samuel Haley house, which is still standing, and the Honvet house, right background, where famous murders were committed in March 1873.

The Honvet house on Smuttynose island. Famous murders were committed here in 1873 but the real interest in the picture is the fish flakes in the foreground. These racks were used to dry the fish as the author explains in this book.

and fascinating and new. We entered the quaint little old stone cottage that was for six years our home. How curious it seemed, with its low, whitewashed ceiling and deep window-seats, showing the great thickness of the walls made to withstand the breakers, with whose force we soon grew acquainted! A blissful home the little house became to the children who entered it that quiet evening and slept for the first time lulled by the murmur of the encircling sea. I do not think a happier triad ever existed than we were, living in that profound isolation. It takes so little to make a healthy child happy; and we never wearied of our few resources. True, the winters seemed as long as a whole year to our little minds, but they were pleasant, nevertheless. Into the deep window-seats we climbed, and with pennies (for which we had no other use) made round holes in the thick frost, breathing on them till they were warm, and peeped out at the bright, fierce, windy weather, watching the vessels scudding over the intensely dark blue sea, all " feather-white " where the short waves broke hissing in the cold, and the sea-fowl soaring aloft or tossing on the water; or, in calmer days, we saw how the stealthy Star-Islander paddled among the ledges, or lay for hours stretched on the wet sea-weed,

6

with his gun, watching for wild-fowl. Sometimes the round head of a seal moved about among the kelp-covered rocks. A few are seen every winter, and are occasionally shot; but they are shyer and more alert even than the birds.

We were forced to lay in stores of all sorts in the autumn, as if we were fitting out a ship for an Arctic expedition. The lower story of the lighthouse was hung with mutton and beef, and the store-room packed with provisions.

In the long, covered walk that bridged the gorge between the lighthouse and the house, we played in stormy days; and every evening it was a fresh excitement to watch the lighting of the lamps, and think how far the lighthouse sent its rays, and how many hearts it gladdened with assurance of safety. As I grew older I was allowed to kindle the lamps sometimes myself. That was indeed a pleasure. So little a creature as I might do that much for the great world! But by the fireside our best pleasure lay, — with plants and singing birds and books and playthings and loving care and kindness the cold and stormy season wore itself at last away, and died into the summer calm. We hardly saw a human face beside our own all winter; but with the spring came manifold life to our lonely dwelling, —human life

among other forms. Our neighbors from Star
rowed across; the pilot-boat from Portsmouth
steered over, and brought us letters, newspapers,
magazines, and told us the news of months. The
faint echoes from the far-off world hardly touched
us little ones. We listened to the talk of our
elders. " Winfield Scott and Santa Anna!" "The
war in Mexico!" "The famine in Ireland!" It
all meant nothing to us. We heard the reading
aloud of details of the famine, and saw tears in
the eyes of the reader, and were vaguely sorry;
but the fate of Red Riding-Hood was much more
near and dreadful to us. We waited for the
spring with an eager longing; the advent of the
growing grass, the birds and flowers and insect
life, the soft skies and softer winds, the everlast-
ing beauty of the thousand tender tints that
clothed the world, — these things brought us un-
speakable bliss. To the heart of Nature one
must needs be drawn in such a life; and very soon
I learned how richly she repays in deep refreshment the reverent love of her worshipper. With
the first warm days we built our little mountains
of wet gravel on the beach, and danced after the
sandpipers at the edge of the foam, shouted to
the gossiping kittiwakes that fluttered above, or
watched the pranks of the burgomaster gull, or

cried to the crying loons. The gannet's long, white wings stretched overhead, perhaps, or the dusky shag made a sudden shadow in mid-air, or we startled on some lonely ledge the great blue heron that flew off, trailing legs and wings, stork-like, against the clouds. Or, in the sunshine on the bare rocks, we cut from the broad, brown leaves of the slippery, varnished kelps, grotesque shapes of man and bird and beast that withered in the wind and blew away; or we fashioned rude boats from bits of driftwood, manned them with a weird crew of kelpies, and set them adrift on the great deep, to float we cared not whither.

We played with the empty limpet-shells; they were mottled gray and brown, like the song-spar-row's breast. We launched fleets of purple mus-sel-shells on the still pools in the rocks, left by the tide, — pools that were like bits of fallen rainbow with the wealth of the sea, with tints of delicate sea-weeds, crimson and green and ruddy brown and violet; where wandered the pearly eolis with rosy spines and fairy horns; and the large, round sea-urchins, like a boss upon a shield, were fastened here and there on the rock at the bottom, putting out from their green, prickly spikes transparent tentacles to seek their invisible food. Rosy and lilac star-fish clung to the sides;

in some dark nook, perhaps, a holothure unfolded its perfect ferns, a lovely, warm buff color, delicate as frost-work; little forests of coralline moss grew up in stillness, gold-colored shells crept about, and now and then flashed the silver-darting fins of slender minnows. The dimmest recesses were haunts of sea-anemones that opened wide their starry flowers to the flowing tide, or drew themselves together, and hung in large, half-transparent drops, like clusters of some strange, amber-colored fruit, along the crevices as the water ebbed away. Sometimes we were cruel enough to capture a female lobster hiding in a deep cleft, with her millions of mottled eggs; or we laughed to see the hermit-crabs challenge each other, and come out and fight a deadly battle till the stronger overcame, and, turning the weaker topsy-turvy, possessed himself of his ampler cockle-shell, and scuttled off with it triumphant. Or, pulling all together, we dragged up the long kelps, or devil's-aprons; their roots were almost always fastened about large, living mussels; these we unclasped, carrying the mussels home to be cooked; fried in crumbs or batter, they were as good as oysters. We picked out from the kelp-roots a kind of star-fish which we called sea-spider; the moment we touched it an extraordinary process began. One by one it disjointed all its sections, — whether from fear or anger we knew not; but it threw itself away, bit by bit, until nothing was left of it save the little, round body whence the legs had sprung!

With crab and limpet, with grasshopper and cricket, we were friends and neighbors, and we were never tired of watching the land-spiders that possessed the place. Their webs covered every window-pane to the lighthouse top, and they rebuilt them as fast as they were swept down. One variety lived among the round gray stones on the beach, just above high-water mark, and spun no webs at all. Large and black, they speckled the light stones, swarming in the hot sun; at the first footfall they vanished beneath the pebbles.

All the cracks in the rocks were draped with swinging veils like the window-panes. How often have we marvelled at them, after a fog or a heavy fall of dew, in the early morning, when every slender thread was strung with glittering drops, — the whole symmetrical web a wonder of shining jewels trembling in the breeze! Tennyson's lines,

> " The cobweb woven across the cannon's throat
> Shall shake its threaded tears in the wind no more,"

always bring back to my mind the memory of

those delicate, spangled draperies, more beautiful than any mortal loom could weave, that curtained the rocks at White Island and "shook their threaded tears" in every wind.

Sometimes we saw the bats wheel through the summer dusk, and in profoundly silent evenings heard, from the lighthouse top, their shrill, small cries, their voices sharper and finer than needle-points. One day I found one clinging to the under side of a shutter, — a soft, dun-colored, downy lump. I took it in my hand, and in an instant it changed to a hideous little demon, and its fierce white teeth met in the palm of my hand. So much fury in so small a beast I never encountered, and I was glad enough to give him his liberty without more ado.

A kind of sandhopper about an inch long, that infested the beach, was a great source of amusement. Lifting the stranded sea-weed that marked the high-water line, we always startled a gray and brown cloud of them from beneath it, leaping away, like tiny kangaroos, out of sight. In storms these were driven into the house, forcing their way through every crack and cranny till they strewed the floors, — the sea so encircled us! Dying immediately upon leaving the water from which they fled, they turned from a clear brown, or what Mr. Kingsley would call a "pellucid gray," to bright brick-color, like a boiled lobster, and many a time I have swept them up in ruddy heaps; they looked like bits of coral.

I remember in the spring kneeling on the ground to seek the first blades of grass that pricked through the soil, and bringing them into the house to study and wonder over. Better than a shop full of toys they were to me! Whence came their color? How did they draw their sweet, refreshing tint from the brown earth, or the limpid air, or the white light? Chemistry was not at hand to answer me, and all her wisdom would not have dispelled the wonder. Later the little scarlet pimpernel charmed me. It seemed more than a flower; it was like a human thing. I knew it by its homely name of poor-man's weather-glass. It was so much wiser than I, for, when the sky was yet without a cloud, softly it clasped its small red petals together, folding its golden heart in safety from the shower that was sure to come! How could it know so much? Here is a question science cannot answer. The pimpernel grows everywhere about the islands, in every cleft and cranny where a suspicion of sustenance for its slender root can lodge; and it is one of the most exquisite of flowers, so rich in color, so quaint and dainty in its method of growth. I never knew its silent warning fail. I wondered much how every flower knew what to do and to be; why the morning-glory did n't forget sometimes, and bear a cluster of elder-bloom, or the elder hang out pennons of gold and purple like the iris, or the golden-rod suddenly blaze out a scarlet plume, the color of the pimpernel, was a mystery to my childish thought. And why did the sweet wild primrose wait till after sunset to unclose its pale yellow buds; why did it unlock its treasure of rich perfume to the night alone? Few flowers bloomed for me upon the lonesome rock; but I made the most of all I had, and neither knew of nor desired more. Ah, how beautiful they were! Tiny stars of crimson sorrel threaded on their long brown stems; the blackberry blossoms in bridal white; the surprise of the blue-eyed grass; the crowfoot flowers, like drops of yellow gold spilt about among the short grass and over the moss; the rich, blue-purple beach-pea, the sweet, spiked germander, and the homely, delightful yarrow that grows thickly on all the islands. Sometimes its broad clusters of dull white bloom are stained a lovely reddish-purple, as if with the light of sunset. I never saw it colored so elsewhere. Quantities of slender, wide-spreading

6*   I

mustard-bushes grew about the house ; their delicate flowers were like fragrant golden clouds.
Dandelions, buttercups, and clover were not de-
nied to us ; though we had no daisies nor violets
nor wild roses, no asters, but gorgeous spikes of
golden-rod, and wonderful wild morning-glories,
whose long, pale, ivory buds I used to find in the
twilight, glimmering among the dark leaves, waiting for the touch of dawn to unfold and become
each an exquisite incarnate blush, — the perfect
color of a South Sea shell.   They ran wild, knot-
ting and twisting about the rocks, and smothering
the loose boulders in the gorges with lush green
leaves and pink blossoms.

Many a summer morning have I crept out of
the still house before any one was awake, and,
wrapping myself closely from the chill wind of
dawn, climbed to the top of the high cliff called
the Head to watch the sunrise.   Pale grew the
lighthouse flame before the broadening day as,
nestled in a crevice at the cliff's edge, I watched
the shadows draw away and morning break.   Facing the east and south, with all the Atlantic before
me, what happiness was mine as the deepening rose-
color flushed the delicate cloudflocks that dappled
the sky, where the gulls soared, rosy too, while the
calm sea blushed beneath.   Or perhaps it was a

cloudless sunrise with a sky of orange-red, and the
sea-line silver-blue against it, peaceful as heaven.
Infinite variety of beauty always awaited me, and
filled me with an absorbing, unreasoning joy such
as makes the song-sparrow sing, — a sense of perfect bliss. Coming back in the sunshine, the morning-glories would lift up their faces, all awake, to
my adoring gaze. Like countless rosy trumpets
sometimes I thought they were, tossed everywhere
about the rocks, turned up to the sky, or droop-
ing toward the ground, or looking east, west,
north, south, in silent loveliness. It seemed as
if they had gathered the peace of the golden morning in their still depths even as my heart had
gathered it.

In some of those matchless summer mornings
when I went out to milk the little dun cow, it was
hardly possible to go farther than the doorstep,
for pure wonder, as I looked abroad at the sea
lying still, like a vast, round mirror, the tide drawn
away from the rich brown rocks, a sail or two
asleep in the calm, not a sound abroad except a
few bird voices ; dew lying like jewel-dust sifted
over everything, — diamond and ruby, sapphire,
topaz, and amethyst, flashing out of the emerald deeps of the tufted grass or from the bending tops. Looking over to the mainland, I could

dimly discern in the level sunshine the depths of
glowing green woods faintly revealed in the distance, fold beyond fold of hill and valley thickly
clothed with the summer's splendor.   But my
handful of grass was more precious to me than
miles of green fields, and I was led to consider
every blade where there were so few.   Not long
ago I had watched them piercing the ground toward
the light ; now, how strong in their slender grace
were these stems, how perfect the poise of the
heavy heads that waved with such harmony of
movement in the faintest breeze !   And I noticed
at mid-day when the dew was dry, where the tall,
blossoming spears stood in graceful companies
that, before they grew purple, brown, and ripe,
when they began to blossom, they put out first a
downy ring of pollen in tiny, yellow rays, held by
an almost invisible thread, which stood out like an
aureole from each slow-waving head, — a fairy-like
effect.   On Seavey's Island (united to ours by a
narrow beach covered at high tide with contending
waves) grew one single root of fern, the only one
within the circle of my little world. It was safe
in a deep cleft, but I was in perpetual anxiety lest
my little cow, going there daily to pasture, should
leave her cropping of the grass and eat it up some
day.   Poor little cow !   One night she did not

come home to be milked as usual, and on going to seek her we found she had caught one foot in a crevice and twisted her hoof entirely off! That was a calamity; for we were forced to summon our neighbors and have her killed on the spot.

I had a scrap of garden, literally not more than a yard square, wherein grew only African marigolds, rich in color as barbaric gold. I knew nothing of John Keats at that time, — poor Keats, "who told Severn that he thought his intensest pleasure in life had been to watch the growth of flowers," — but I am sure he never felt their beauty more devoutly than the little, half-savage being who knelt, like a fire-worshipper, to watch the unfolding of those golden disks. When, later, the "brave new world" of poets was opened to me, with what power those glowing lines of his went straight to my heart,

> " Open afresh your rounds of starry folds,
> Ye ardent marigolds! "

All flowers had for me such human interest, they were so dear and precious, I hardly liked to gather them, and when they were withered, I carried them all to one place and laid them tenderly together, and never liked to pass the spot where they were hidden.

Once or twice every year came the black, lumbering old "oil-schooner" that brought supplies for the lighthouse, and the inspector, who gravely examined everything, to see if all was in order. He left stacks of clear red and white glass chimneys for the lamps, and several doe-skins for polishing the great, silver-lined copper reflectors, large bundles of wicks, and various pairs of scissors for trimming them, heavy black casks of ill-perfumed whale-oil, and other things, which were all stowed in the round, dimly-lighted rooms of the tower. Very awe-struck, we children always crept into corners, and whispered and watched the intruders till they embarked in their ancient, clumsy vessel, and, hoisting their dark, weather-stained sails, bore slowly away again. About ten years ago that old white lighthouse was taken away, and a new, perpendicular brick tower built in its place. The lantern, with its fifteen lamps, ten golden and five red, gave place to Fresnel's powerful single burner, or, rather, three burners in one, enclosed in its case of prisms. The old lighthouse was by far the most picturesque; but perhaps the new one is more effective, the light being, undoubtedly, more powerful.

Often, in pleasant days, the head of the family sailed away to visit the other islands, sometimes taking the children with him, oftener going alone, frequently not returning till after dark. The land-

ing at White Island is so dangerous that the greatest care is requisite, if there is any sea running, to
get ashore in safety. Two long and very solid timbers about three feet apart are laid from the boat-
house to low-water mark, and between those timbers the boat's bow must be accurately steered; if
she goes to the right or the left, woe to her crew
unless the sea is calm! Safely lodged in the slip,
as it is called, she is drawn up into the boat-house
by a capstan, and fastened securely. The lighthouse gave no ray to the dark rock below it; sending its beams far out to sea, it left us at its foot in
greater darkness for its lofty light. So when the
boat was out late, in soft, moonless summer nights,
I used to light a lantern, and, going down to the
water's edge, take my station between the timbers
of the slip, and, with the lantern at my feet, sit
waiting in the darkness, quite content, knowing
my little star was watched for, and that the safety
of the boat depended in a great measure upon it.
How sweet the summer wind blew, how softly
plashed the water round me, how refreshing was
the odor of the sparkling brine! High above, the
lighthouse rays streamed out into the humid dark,
and the cottage windows were ruddy from the glow
within. I felt so much a part of the Lord's
universe, I was no more afraid of the dark than the

waves or winds; but I was glad to hear at last the creaking of the mast and the rattling of the row-locks as the boat approached; and, while yet she was far off, the lighthouse touched her one large sail into sight, so that I knew she was nearing me, and shouted, listening for the reply that came so blithely back to me over the water.

Unafraid, too, we watched the summer tempests, and listened to the deep, melodious thunder rolling away over the rain-calmed ocean. The lightning played over the iron rods that ran from the lighthouse-top down into the sea. Where it lay on the sharp ridgepole of the long, covered walk that spanned the gorge, the strange fire ran up the spikes that were set at equal distances, and burnt like pale flame from their tips. It was fine indeed from the lighthouse itself to watch the storm come rushing over the sea and ingulf us in our help-lessness. How the rain weltered down over the great panes of plate glass, — floods of sweet, fresh water that poured off the rocks and mingled with the bitter brine. I wondered why the fresh floods never made the salt sea any sweeter. Those pale flames that we beheld burning from the spikes of the lightning-rod, I suppose were identical with the St. Elmo's fire that I have since seen described as haunting the spars of ships in thunder-storms.

And here I am reminded of a story told by some gentlemen visiting Appledore sixteen or eighteen years ago. They started from Portsmouth for the Shoals in a whaleboat, one evening in summer, with a native Star-Islander, Richard Randall by name, to manage the boat. They had sailed about half the distance, when they were surprised at seeing a large ball of fire, like a rising moon, rolling toward them over the sea from the south. They watched it eagerly as it bore down upon them, and, veering off, went east of them at some little distance, and then passed astern, and there, of course, they expected to lose sight of it; but while they were marvelling and speculating, it altered its course, and suddenly began to near them, coming back upon its track against the wind and steadily following in their wake. This was too much for the native Shoaler. He took off his jacket and turned it inside out to exorcise the fiend, and lo, the apparition most certainly disappeared! We heard the excited account of the strange gentlemen and witnessed the holy horror of the boatman on the occasion; but no one could imagine what had set the globe of fire rolling across the sea. Some one suggested that it might be an exhalation, a phosphorescent light, from the decaying body of some dead fish; but in that case it must have been taken in tow by some living finny creature, else how could it have sailed straight "into the teeth of the wind"? It was never satisfactorily accounted for, and must remain a mystery.

One autumn at White Island our little boat had been to Portsmouth for provisions, etc. With the spy-glass we watched her returning, beating against the head wind. The day was bright, but there had been a storm at sea, and the breakers rolled and roared about us. The process of "beating" is so tedious that, though the boat had started in the morning, the sun was sending long yellow light from the west before it reached the island. There was no cessation in those resistless billows that rolled from the Devil's Rock upon the slip; but still the little craft sailed on, striving to reach the landing. The hand at the tiller was firm, but a huge wave swept suddenly in, swerving the boat to the left of the slip, and in a moment she was overturned and flung upon the rocks, and her only occupant tossed high upon the beach, safe except for a few bruises; but what a moment of terror it was for us all, who saw and could not save! All the freight was lost except a roll of iron wire and a barrel of walnuts. These were spread on the floor of an unoccupied eastern chamber in the cottage to dry. And they did dry; but before they were gathered up came a terrible storm from the southeast. It raved and tore at lighthouse and cottage; the sea broke into the windows of that eastern chamber where the walnuts lay, and washed them out till they came dancing down the stairs in briny foam! The sea broke the windows of the house several times during our stay at the lighthouse. Everything shook so violently from the concussion of the breakers, that dishes on the closet shelves fell to the floor, and one member of the family was at first always made sea-sick in storms, by the tremor and deafening confusion. One night when, from the southeast, the very soul of chaos seemed to have been let loose upon the world, the whole ponderous "walk" (the covered bridge that connected the house and lighthouse) was carried thundering down the gorge and dragged out into the raging sea.

It was a distressing situation for us, — cut off from the precious light that must be kept alive; for the breakers were tearing through the gorge so that no living thing could climb across. But the tide could not resist the mighty impulse that drew it down; it was forced to obey the still voice that bade it ebb; all swollen and raging and towering as it was, slowly and surely, at the appointed time, it sank away from our rock, so that, between the billows that still strove to clutch at the white, silent, golden-crowned tower, one could creep across, and scale the height, and wind up the machinery that kept the great clustered light revolving till the gray daylight broke to extinguish it.

I often wondered how it was possible for the sea-birds to live through such storms as these. But, when one could see at all, the gulls were always soaring, in the wildest tumult, and the stormy petrels half flying, half swimming in the hollows of the waves.

Would it were possible to describe the beauty of the calm that followed such tempests! The long lines of silver foam that streaked the tranquil blue, the "tender-curving lines of creamy spray" along the shore, the clear-washed sky, the peaceful yellow light, the mellow breakers murmuring slumberously!

Of all the storms our childish eyes watched with delighted awe, one thunder-storm remains fixed in my memory. Late in an August afternoon it rolled its awful clouds to the zenith, and, after the tumult had subsided, spread its lightened vapors in an under-roof of gray over all the sky. Presently this solemn gray lid was lifted at its

western edge, and an insufferable splendor streamed
across the world from the sinking sun. The
whole heaven was in a blaze of scarlet, across
which sprang a rainbow unbroken to the topmost
clouds, " with its seven perfect colors chorded in a
triumph " against the flaming background; the
sea answered the sky's rich blush, and the gray
rocks lay drowned in melancholy purple. I hid
my face from the glory, — it was too much to
bear. Ever I longed to *speak* these things that
made life so sweet, to speak the wind, the cloud,
the bird's flight, the sea's murmur. A vain longing! I might as well have sighed for the mighty
pencil of Michael Angelo to wield in my impotent
child's hand. Better to " hush and bless one's
self with silence"; but ever the wish grew. Facing the July sunsets, deep red and golden through
and through, or watching the summer northern
lights, — battalions of brilliant streamers advancing and retreating, shooting upward to the zenith,
and glowing like fiery veils before the stars; or
when the fog-bow spanned the silver mist of
morning, or the earth and sea lay shimmering in a
golden haze of noon; in storm or calm, by day or
night, the manifold aspects of Nature held me
and swayed all my thoughts until it was impossible to be silent any longer, and I was fain to

mingle my voice with her myriad voices, only aspiring to be in accord with the Infinite harmony,
however feeble and broken the notes might be.

It has been my good fortune to witness but few
wrecks at the Shoals. The disasters of which we
hear faintly from the past were many and dreadful; but since the building of the lighthouse on
White Island, and also on Boone Island (which
seems like a neighbor, though fifteen miles distant), the danger of the place is much lessened.
A resident of Star Island told me of a wreck which
took place forty-seven years ago, during a heavy
storm from the eastward. It blew so that all the
doors in the house opened as fast as they shut
them, and in the night a vessel drove against
"Hog Island Head," which fronts the village on
Star. She went to pieces utterly. In the morning the islanders perceived the beach at Londoners
heaped with some kind of drift; they could not
make out what it was, but, as soon as the sea subsided, went to examine and found a mass of
oranges and picture-frames, with which the vessel
had been freighted. Not a soul was saved. "She
struck with such force that she drove a large
spike out of her forefoot" into a crevice in the
rock, which was plainly to be seen till a few years

ago. My informant also told me that she remembered the wreck of the Sagunto, in 1813 ; that the
beaches were strewn with "almond-nuts" long after;
and that she picked up curiously embroidered vests
and "work-bags" in all directions along the shores.

During a storm in 1839, while living at White
Island, we were startled by the heavy booming of
guns through the roar of the tempest, — a sound
that drew nearer and nearer, till at last, through a
sudden break in the mist and spray, we saw the
heavily rolling hull of a large vessel driving by, to
her sure destruction, toward the coast. It was as
if the wind had torn the vapor apart on purpose
to show us this piteous sight ; and I well remember the hand on my shoulder which held me firmly,
shuddering child that I was, and forced me to look
in spite of myself. What a day of pain it was!
how dreadful the sound of those signal-guns, and
how much more dreadful the certainty, when they
ceased, that all was over! We learned afterward
that it was the brig Pocahontas, homeward bound
from Spain, and that the vessel and all her crew
were lost. In later years a few coasters and fishermen have gone ashore at the islands, generally
upon the hidden ledges at Duck. Many of these
have been loaded with lime, — a most perilous
freight ; for as soon as the water touches it there is

a double danger ; and between fire and water there is little chance of escape.

I wish I could recall the graphic language of a Star Islander who described to me a wreck of this kind. The islanders saw at sunrise, one bitter winter day, a schooner ashore among the dreadful ledges at Duck Island, and, though the wind blew half a gale, they took their boats and ran down toward her before the northwester. Smoke and steam and spray and flame were rising from her and about her when they reached the spot. Only one man was found alive. From the davits, hanging head downward, was the lifeless body of a fair-haired boy of sixteen or thereabouts. The breakers swept him to and fro, and, drawing away, left his long yellow hair dripping with the freezing brine. The mate's story was that he had gone to unfasten the boat which hung at the stern, that a sea had struck him, and he had fallen headforemost with his feet entangled in the ropes of the davits. He was the only son of his mother, who was a widow. They carried his body home to that most unhappy mother. The vessel was a total loss, with all on board, except the mate.

One winter night at Appledore when it was blowing very hard northwest, with a clear sky, we were wakened by a violent knocking at the door. So unaccustomed a sound, at that time of night too, was enough to startle us all, and very much amazed we were. The door was opened to admit four or five shipwrecked men, whose hands, feet, and ears were all frozen stiff, — pitiable objects they were indeed. Their vessel had struck full on York Ledge, a rock lying off the coast of Maine far east of us, and they had taken to the boat and strove to make a landing on the coast ; but the wind blew off shore so fiercely they failed in their attempt, their hands became useless from the cold, they dropped their oars, and, half steering with one of the seats of the boat, managed to reach Appledore, more dead than alive. They were obliged to remain there several days before finding an opportunity of going on shore, the gale was so furious. Next morning, in the glare of the winter sunshine, we saw their vessel, still with all sail set, standing upright upon the ledge, — a white column looming far away. One of the most hideous experiences I have heard befell a young Norwegian now living at the Shoals. He and a young companion came out from Portsmouth to set their trawl, in the winter fishing, two years ago. Before they reached the island, came a sudden squall of wind and snow, chilling and blinding. In a few moments they knew not

7   J

where they were, and the wind continued to sweep them away. Presently they found themselves under the lee of White Island Head; they threw out the road-lines of their trawl, in desperate hope that they might hold the boat till the squall abated. The keepers at the lighthouse saw the poor fellows, but were powerless to help them. Alas! the road-lines soon broke, and the little boat was swept off again, they knew not whither. Night came down upon them, tossed on that terrible black sea; the snow ceased, the clouds flew before the deadly cold northwest wind, the thermometer sank below zero. One of the men died before morning; the other, alone with the dead man, was still driven on and on before the pitiless gale. He had no cap nor mittens; had lost both. He bailed the boat incessantly, for the sea broke over him the livelong time. He told me the story himself. He looked down at the awful face of his dead friend and thought "how soon he should be like him"; but still he never ceased bailing, — it was all he could do. Before night he passed Cape Cod and knew it as he rushed by. Another unspeakably awful night, and the gale abated no whit. Next morning he was almost gone from cold, fatigue, and hunger. His eyes were so swollen he could hardly see; but afar off, shining whiter than silver in the sun, the sails of a large schooner appeared at the edge of the fearful wilderness. He managed to hoist a bit of old canvas on an oar. He was then not far from Holmes' Hole, nearly two hundred miles from the Shoals! The schooner saw it and bore down for him, but the sea was running so high that he expected to be swamped every instant. As she swept past, they threw from the deck a rope with a loop at the end, tied with a bow-line knot that would not slip. It caught him over the head, and clutching it at his throat with both hands, in an instant he found himself in the sea among the ice-cold, furious waves, drawn toward the vessel with all the strength of her crew. Just before he emerged, he heard the captain shout, "We've lost him!" Ah the bitter moment! For a horrible fear struck through him that they might lose their hold an instant on the rope, and then he knew it would be all over. But they saved him. The boat with the dead man in it, all alone, went tossing, heaven knows where.

The great equinoctial gale of September 8, 1869, was very severe at the islands. One schooner went ashore on Cannon Point at Appledore, and was a complete wreck, though no lives were lost. She was lying in "The Roads," between Star and Appledore, safely moored, her crew supposed; but she dragged moorings, anchors, everything with which they strove to save her, and crashed on the rocks, breaking up like an eggshell. Various buildings were blown down; windows at Appledore were blown in, in some cases sash and all, in others the glass was smashed as if the wind had thrust an arm through.

At about seven o'clock in the evening a great copper-colored arch spanned the black sky from west to east. The gale was then at its height. After that lurid bow dissolved, flying northward in wild, scattered fragments, the wind abated, and we began to take breath again. A man at Star, on the edge of the storm, rowed out in his dory to make more secure a larger boat moored at a little distance. Down came the hurricane and caught him, and whirled him away like a dead leaf on the surface of the sea. He gave himself up for lost, of course; so did his friends. But he fastened himself with ropes to the inside of the boat, and, tossing from billow to billow, bailed for dear life the whole night long. Toward morning, the wind lulling very considerably, he was carried along the coast of Maine, and landed in York, a short distance from his father's home, and quietly walked into the house and joined the family at breakfast; then took the cars for Portsmouth, and astounded the whole Shoals settlement by appearing in the steamer Appledore in time for dinner. Everybody supposed him, without a shadow of doubt, to be at the bottom of the sea.

Boone Island is the forlornest place that can be imagined. The Isles of Shoals, barren as they are, seem like Gardens of Eden in comparison. I chanced to hear last summer of a person who had been born and brought up there; he described the loneliness as something absolutely fearful, and declared it had pursued him all through his life. He lived there till fourteen or fifteen years old, when his family moved to York. While living on the island he discovered some human remains which had lain there thirty years. A carpenter and his assistants, having finished some building, were capsized in getting off, and all were drowned, except the master. One body floated to Plum Island at the mouth of the Merrimack; the others the master secured, made a box for them, -- all alone the while, — and buried them in a cleft and covered them with stones. These stones the sea washed away, and, thirty years after they were buried, the boy found the bones, which were re-moved to York and there buried again. It was on board a steamer bound to Bangor, that the man told his story. Boone Island Light was shining in the distance. He spoke with bitterness of his life in that terrible solitude, and of " the loneliness which had pursued him ever since." All his relatives were dead, he said, and he had no human tie in the wide world except his wife. He ended by anathematizing all islands, and, vanishing into the darkness, was not to be found again ; nor did his name or any trace of him transpire, though he was sought for in the morning all about the vessel.

One of the most shocking stories of shipwreck I remember to have heard is that of the Nottingham Galley, wrecked on this island in the year 1710. There is a narrative of this shipwreck existing, written by " John Deane, then commander of said Galley, but for many years after his Majesty's consul for the ports of Flanders, residing at Ostend," printed in 1762. The ship, of one hundred and twenty tons, carrying ten guns, with a crew of fourteen men, loaded partly in England and partly in Ireland, and sailed for Boston on the 25th of September, 1710. She made land on the 11th of December, and was wrecked on that fatal rock. At first the unhappy crew " treated each other with kindness and condolence, and prayed to God for relief." The only things saved from the wreck were a bit of canvas and half a cheese. The men made a triangular tent of the bit of canvas, and all lay close together beneath it, sideways; none could turn without the general concurrence : they turned once in two hours upon public notice. They had no fire, and lived upon kelp and rock-weed, and mussels, three a day to a man. Starvation and suffering soon produced a curious loss of memory. The fourth day the cook died. When they had been there upwards of a week, they saw three sails in the southwest, but no boat came near them. They built a rude boat of such materials as they could gather from the wreck, but she was lost in launching. One of the men, a Swede, is particularly mentioned ; he seems to have been full of energy ; with help from the others he built a raft ; in launching this they overset it. Again they saw a sail, this time coming out from the Piscataqua River ; it was soon out of sight. The Swede was determined to make an effort to reach the shore, and persuaded another man to make the attempt with him. At sunset they were seen half-way to the land ; the raft was found on shore with the body of one man ; the Swede was never seen more. A hide was thrown on the rocks at Boone Island by the sea ;. this the poor sailors ate raw, minced. About the end of December the carpenter died, and, driven to madness by hunger, they devoured the flesh of their dead comrade. The captain, being the strongest of the party, dragged the body away and hid it, and dealt small portions of it daily to the men. Immediately their dispositions underwent a horrible change. They became fierce and reckless, and were the most pitiable objects of despair, when, on January 4th, 1711, they were discovered and taken off. It was evening when they entered the Piscataqua River, and eight o'clock when they landed. Discovering a house through the darkness, the master rushed into it, frightening the gentlewoman and children desperately, and, making his way to the kitchen, snatched the pot wherein some food was cooking off the fire, and began to eat voraciously. This old record mentions John Plaisted and John Wentworth as being most " forward in benevolence " to these poor fellows.

When visiting the island for the first time, a few years ago, I was shown the shallow gorge where the unfortunates tried to shelter themselves. It was the serenest of summer days ; everything smiled and shone as I stood looking down into that rocky hollow. Near by the lighthouse sprang — a splendid piece of masonry — over a hundred feet into the air, to hold its warning aloft. About its base some gentle thought had caused morning-glories to climb and unfold their violet, white, and rosy bells against the smooth, dark stone. I thought I had never seen flowers so beautiful. There was hardly a handful of grass on the island, hardly soil enough to hold a root; therefore it seemed the more wonderful to behold this lovely apparition. With my mind full of the story of the Nottingham Galley, I looked at the delicate bells, the cool green leaves, the whole airy grace of the wandering vines, and it was as if a hand were stretched out to pluck me away from the awful questions never to be answered this side the grave, that pressed so heavily while I thought how poor humanity had here suffered the utmost misery that it is possible to endure.

The aspect of this island from the Shoals is very striking, so lonely it lies on the eastern horizon, its tall lighthouse like a slender column against the sky. It is easily mistaken for the smoke-stack of a steamer by unaccustomed eyes, and sometimes the watcher most familiar with its appearance can hardly distinguish it from the distant white sails that steal by it, to and fro. Sometimes it looms colossal in the mirage of summer; in winter it lies blurred and ghostly at the edge of chilly sea and pallid sky. In the sad, strange light of winter sunsets, its faithful star blazes sud-

7*

denly from the darkening east, and sends a friendly ray across to its neighbor at the Shoals, waiting as it also waits, ice-bound, storm-swept, and solitary, for gentler days to come. And "winter's rains and ruins" have an end at last.

In the latter part of February, after ten days perhaps of the northwester, bringing across to the islands all the chill of the snow-covered hills of the continent, some happy evening it dies into a reasonable breeze, and, while the sun sets, you climb the snowy height, and sweep with your eyes the whole circle of the horizon, with nothing to impede the view. Ah! how sad it looks in the dying light! Star Island close by with its silent little village and the sails of belated fishing-boats hurrying in over the dark water to the moorings; White Island afar off "kindling its great red star"; on every side the long, bleached points of granite stretching out into the sea, so cold and bleak; the line of coast, sad purple; and the few schooners leaden and gray in the distance. Yet there is a hopeful glow where the sun went down, suggestive of the spring; and before the ruddy sweetness of the western sky the melancholy east is flushed with violet, and up into the delicious color rolls a gradual moon, mellow and golden as in harvest-time, while high above her the great star Jupiter begins to glitter clear. On such an evening some subtle influence of the coming spring steals to the heart, and eyes that have watched the winter skies so patiently grow wistful with the thought of summer days to come. On shore in these last weeks of winter one becomes aware, by various delicate tokens, of the beautiful change at hand, — by the deepening of the golden willow wands into a more living color, and by their silvery buds, which in favored spots burst the brown sheaths; by the reddening of bare maple-trees, as if with promise of future crimson flowers; by the sweet cry of the returning bluebird; by the alders at the river's edge. If the season is mild, the catkins begin to unwind their tawny tresses in the first weeks of March. But here are no trees, and no bluebirds come till April. Perhaps some day the delightful clangor of the wild geese is heard, and looking upward, lo! the long, floating ribbon streaming northward across the sky. What joy they bring to hearts so weary with waiting! Truly a wondrous content is shaken down with their wild clamors out of the cloudy heights, and a courage and vigor lurk in these strong voices that touch the listener with something better than gladness, while he traces eagerly the wavering lines that seek the north with steady, measured flight.

Gradually the bitter winds abate; early in March the first flocks of crows arrive, and they soar finely above the coves, and perch on the flukes of stranded anchors or the tops of kellock-sticks that lie about the water's edge. They are most welcome, for they are never seen in winter; and pleasant it is to watch them beating their black, ragged pinions in the blue, while the gulls swim on beyond them serenely, shining still whiter for their sable color. No other birds come till about the 27th of March, and then all at once the islands are alive with song-sparrows, and these sing from morning till night so beautifully that dull and weary indeed must be the mortal who can resist the charm of their fresh music. There is a matchless sweetness and good cheer in this brave bird. The nightingale singing with its breast against a thorn may be divine; yet would I turn away from its tender melody to listen to the fresh, cheerful, healthy song of this dauntless and happy little creature. They come in flocks to be fed every morning the whole summer long, tame and charming, with their warm brown and gray feathers, striped and freaked with wood-color, and little brown knots at each pretty throat! They build their nests, and remain till the snow falls; frequently they remain all winter; sometimes they come into the house for shelter; once one fluttered in and entered the canaries' cage voluntarily, and stayed there singing like a voice from heaven all winter. Robins and blackbirds appear with the sparrows; a few blackbirds build and remain; the robins, finding no trees, flit across to the mainland. Yellow-birds and kingbirds occasionally build here, but very rarely. By the first of April the snow is gone, and our bit of earth is free from that dead white mask. How lovely then the gentle neutral tints of tawny intervals of dead grass and brown bushes and varying stone appear, set in the living sea! There is hardly a square foot of the bare rock that is n't precious for its soft coloring; and freshly beautiful are the uncovered lichens that with patient fingering have ornamented the rough surfaces with their wonderful embroideries. They flourish with the greatest vigor by the sea; whole houses at Star used to be covered with the orange-colored variety, and I have noticed the same thing in the pretty fishing village of Newcastle and on some of the old buildings by the river-side in sleepy Portsmouth city. Through April the weather softens daily, and by the 20th come gray, quiet days with mild northeast wind; in the hollows the grass has greened, and now the gentle color seems to brim over and spread out

upon the ground in faint and fainter gradations.
A refreshing odor springs from the moist earth,
from the short, sweet turf which the cattle crop so
gladly, — a musky fragrance unlike that of inland
pastures; and with this is mingled the pure sea-
breeze, — a most reviving combination.   The turfy
gorges, boulder-strewn and still, remind one of
Alexander Smith's descriptions of his summer in
Skye, of those quiet, lonely glens, — just such a
grassy carpet was spread in their hollows.   By the
23d of April come the first swallow and flocks of
martins, golden-winged and downy woodpeckers,
the tiny, ruby-crowned wren, and troops of many
other kinds of birds; kingfishers that perch on
stranded kellocks, little nuthatches that peck
among the shingles for hidden spiders, and gladden the morning with sweet, quaint cries, so busy
and bright and friendly!   All these tarry only
awhile in their passage to the mainland.

But though the birds come and the sky has re-
lented and grown tender with its melting clouds,
the weather in New England has a fashion of
leaping back into midwinter in the space of an
hour, and all at once comes half a hurricane from
the northwest, charged with the breath of all the
remaining snow-heaps on the far mountain
ranges, — a "white-sea roarin' wind" that takes

you back to January. In the afternoon, through the cold, transparent heaven, a pale half-moon glides slowly over; there is a splendor of wild clouds at sunset, dusk heaps with scarlet fringes, scattered flecks of flame in a clear crimson air above the fallen sun; then cold moonlight over the black sea, with the flash and gleam of white waves the whole night long.

But the potent spirit of the spring triumphs at last. When the sun in its journey north passes a certain group of lofty pine-trees standing out distinctly against the sky on Breakfast Hill in Greenland, New Hampshire, which lies midway in the coast line, then the Shoalers are happy in the conviction that there will be "settled weather"; and they put no trust in any relenting of the elements before that time. After this there soon come days when to be alive is quite enough joy, — days when it is bliss only to watch and feel how

> " God renews
> His ancient rapture," —

days when the sea lies, colored like a turquoise, blue and still, and from the south a band of warm, gray-purple haze steals down on the horizon like an encircling arm about the happy world. The lightest film encroaches upon the sea, only made perceptible by the shimmering of far-off sails. A kind of bloom, inexpressibly lovely, softens over the white canvas of nearer vessels, like a delicate veil. There is a fascination in the motion of these slender schooners, a wondrous grace, as they glide before a gentle wind, slowly bowing, bending, turning, with curving canvas just filled with the breeze, and shadows falling soft from sail to sail. They are all so picturesque, so suggestive, from the small, tanned spritsail some young islander spreads to flit to and fro among the rocks and ledges, to the stately column of canvas that bears the great ship round the world. The variety of their aspects is endless and ever beautiful, whether you watch them from the lighthouse-top, dreaming afar on the horizon, or at the water's edge ; whether they are drowned in the flood of sunshine on the waves, or glide darkly through the track of the moonlight, or fly toward you full of promise, wing and wing, like some magnificent bird, or steal away reddening in the sunset as if to

" Sink with all you love below the verge."

I know nothing sadder than their aspect in the light of the winter sunsets, as they vanish in the cold east, blushing for a fleeting moment, sweetly, faintly, under the last touch of the dropping day. To a child's imagination they are all full of charm and of mystery, freighted with heavenly dreams. "The thoughts of youth are long, long thoughts," and the watching of the sails filled the lonely, lovely summer days of one young Shoaler with joy enough and to spare. How many pictures linger in my mind, — splendid, stately apparitions of full-rigged, slender schooners, passing very near early in the breezy mornings of spring, every inch of canvas in a blaze of white light, and the whole vessel alive from keel to topmast. And well I remember on soft May evenings how they came dropping down from Cape Ann, while the sunset, streaming through low bars of cloud, just touched them with pale gold, and made them half luminous and altogether lovely; and how the fog clung in silver strips to the dark, wet sails of vessels lying becalmed when all the air about was clear and free from mist; how the mackerel fleet surrounded the islands, five hundred craft sometimes between the islands and the coast, so that one might almost walk on shore from deck to deck. It was wonderful to wake on some midsummer morning and find the sea gray-green, like translucent chrysoprase, and the somewhat stormy sunrise painting the sails bright flame-color as they flew before the warm, wild wind that blew strongly from the south. At night, sometimes, in a glory of moonlight, a vessel passed

K

close in with all sail set, and only just air enough
to fill the canvas, enough murmur from the full
tide to drown the sound of her movement, — a
beautiful ghost stealing softly by, and passing in
mysterious light beyond the glimmering headland
out of sight. Here was suggestion enough for
a night full of visions ! Then the scudding of
sails before a storm, — how they came rushing
in from the far, dim sea-line, racing by to Portsmouth Harbor, close-reefed, or under darkened
mainsail and jib only, leaping over the long swell,
and plunging their sharp bowsprits into a cloud
of snowy spray at every leap ! Then when the
storm had spent itself, how beautiful to see them
stealing tranquilly forth from the river's mouth,
flocking seaward again, shining white in the peaceful morning sunshine ! Watching them in all
their endless variety, coming and going, dreaming,
drifting, or flying, many a time these quaint old
rhymes occurred to me : —

> " Ships, ships, I will descrie you
>   Amidst the main,
> I will come and try you
> What you are protecting,
> And projecting,
>   What 's your end and aim ?
> Some go abroad for merchandise and trading,
> Another stays to keep his country from invading,
> A third is coming home with rich and wealthy lading.
>   Halloo ! my fancie, whither wilt thou go ? "

As the winter is doubly hard, so are the gentler seasons doubly sweet and delightful, when one is shut out with them, as it were, and forced to observe all their changes and peculiarities, with so few human interests to interrupt one's intercourse with nature. The rainy days in May at the Isles of Shoals have seemed to me more lovely than the sunshine in Paradise could be, so charming it was to walk in the warm showers over our island, and note all the mosses and lichens drenched and bright with the moisture, thick, sweet buds on the bayberry bushes, rich green leaves unfolding here and there among the tangled vines, and bright anemones growing up between. The lovely eye-bright glimmers everywhere. The rain, if it continues for several days, bleaches the sea-weed about the shores to a lighter and more golden brown, the sea is gray, and the sky lowers; but all these neutral tints are gentle and refreshing. The coasters rock lazily on the long swell toward Cape Ann, dim through low-hanging clouds; clearly the sandpipers call, and always the song-sparrows freshly surprise you with their outburst of cheerful music. In the last weeks of May comes a period of balmy days, with a gentle, incessant southwest wind, the sea a wonderful gray-blue, with the faint, impalpable haze lying over sails, islands, sea, and coast.   A brooding warmth is everywhere.   The sky is cloudless, but opaque, — a kind of milky effect in the atmosphere, through which the sun is seen as through smoked glass, and long before it sets one can bear to look at the crimson ball slow sinking in the rich, red west; and the moon is like copper, throwing no light on the water.   The islanders call this a "smoky sou'wester."   Now come delicious twilights, with silence broken only by mysterious murmurs from the waves, and sweet, full cries from the sand-pipers fluttering about their nests on the margin of the beaches, — tender, happy notes that thrill the balmy air, and echo softly about the silent, moonlit coves.   Sails in this twilight atmosphere gather the dusk within their folds; if the warm wind is blowing softly, there is enchantment in the sound of the lazily-flapping canvas and in the long creak of the mast.   A human voice borne through this breathing wind comes like a waft of music faintly heard across the water.   The mornings now are exquisite, the delicate flush of the sunrise through this beautiful haze is indescribable. The island is indeed like

" A precious stone set in the silver sea,"

so freshly green, so flower-strewn and fragrant, so

musical with birds, and with the continual caressing of summer waves. Now and then a bobolink
pays us a flying visit, and, tilting on a blackberry
spray, pours out his intoxicating song; some
morning is heard the fairy bugling of an oriole;
a scarlet tanager honors the place with half a day's
sojourn, to be the wonder of all eyes; but com-
monly the swallows hold it in undisputed posses-
sion. The air is woven through and through with
the gleam of their burnished wings and their clear,
happy cries. They are so tame, knowing how
well they are beloved, that they gather on the
window-sills, twittering and fluttering, gay and
graceful, turning their heads this way and that,
eying you askance without a trace of fear. All
day they build their nests about the eaves, nor
heed how loving eyes do watch their charming
toil. Walking abroad in these pleasant evenings,
many a little sparrow's nest one finds low down in
the bayberry-bushes, — smooth, brown cups of woven grass, wherein lie the five speckled eggs, each
full of silent music, each dumb miracle waiting for
the finger of God to wake, to be alive, to drink the
sunshine and the breeze, to fill the air with blissful sound. At the water's edge one finds the
long ledges covered with barnacles, and from each
rough shell a tiny, brown, filmy hand is thrust out,

opening and shutting in gladness beneath the coming tide, feeling the freshness of the flowing water. The shore teems with life in manifold forms. As the darkness gathers, the ripples begin to break in pale flame against the rocks; if the tide is low enough, it is charming to steal down in the shadow, and, drawing aside the curtain of coarse sea-weed that drapes the face of some smooth rock, to write on the surface beneath: the strange fire follows your finger; and there is your name in weird flame, all alive, quivering and trembling, and finally fading and disappearing. In a still pool you drop a stone or touch the water with your hand: instantly a thousand stars break out and burn and vanish in a moment! It used to be a pleasant thing to bring a piece of drift-wood, water-soaked, and shaggy with fine sea-weed, up from the shore, and from some dark corner suddenly sweep my hand across it: a sheet of white flame followed, startling the beholder.

June is of course the most delightful month here, everything is yet so fresh; later the hot sun dries and scorches the thin soil, and partially destroys the little vegetation which finds room upon the island. But through this month the ground is beautiful with starry, purple stone-wort; like little suns the blossoms of the lion's-

foot shine in the thinnest of the soil; herb-robert
blossoms; the slender arenaria steals up among
the bushes, lifting a little white flower to the
sun; here and there the sorrel lies in crimson
stains; in wet places sturdy clumps of fern
unroll their golden green with splendid vigor of
growth; sundew and partridge-berry creep at
their feet; and from the swamp the rushes rise in
ranks, like a faint, green vapor, slowly, day by day.
The few wild-cherry bushes have each its inevi-
table caterpillars' nest; one can but wonder how
caterpillars and canker-worms find their way across
the water. The presence of green snakes on these
rocks may be explained by their having been found
coiled on a piece of drift-wood many miles out at
sea. Bees find their way out from the land in
companies, seeking the white clover-blossoms that
rise in cool, creamy, fragrant globes through the
dark leaves and grass. The clover here is pecul-
iarly rich. Many varieties of butterflies abound,
the handsome moth of the American silkworm
among them. One night in June, at sunset, we
were kindling the lamps in the lighthouse, and
because it was so mild and still outside, the little
iron door of the lantern was left open. No breeze
came in to stir the flame that quivered in the
centre of each shining reflector, but presently

glided through the door the pale-green, exquisite Luna moth, with its wonderful crescents, its lines of velvet brown, and long under wings drawn out like the tail of a swallow. It sailed slowly round and round the dome above the lamps at first, but soon became agitated, and would have dashed itself against the flames but that I caught it. What a marvel it was! I never dreamed of the existence of so beautiful a creature. Titania herself could not have been more interesting to me.

In the quiet little coves troops of butterflies are often seen, anchored for the night, clinging to the thistle-blossoms to be safe from assailing winds. Crickets are never heard here till after the 1st of August. On the mainland they begin, about the 28th of May, a sad and gentle autumnal undertone, which from that time accompanies the jubilant chorus of summer in a gradual *crescendo*, till finally the days pass on to no other music save their sweet, melancholy chirrup. In August comes the ruby-throated humming-bird, and several pairs flutter about the little gardens for weeks. By the 1st of July the wild roses blossom, and every bit of swampy ground is alive with the waving flags of the iris, each flower of which is full of exquisite variety of tint and shade of gold and violet. All over the island patches of it diversify the surface, set like amethysts in the rich greens and browns of turf and mossy spaces. Through the tangle of leaves and grasses the spikes of golden-rod make their way upward slowly day by day, to be ready at the first beckoning of Autumn's finger to light their torches and join the fair procession; the green hollows are filled with blossoming elder, white as a lake of milk; the pimpernel is awake; and the heavy, stout stalks of the mulleins uprear their woolly buds, that soon will break into squares of pallid gold. The world is at high tide of delight. Along the coast-line the mirage races in flowing undulations of heat, changing the hill ranges into a solid wall, to dissolve them, and again reunite them into clusters of gigantic towers and battlements; trees, spires, chimneys, lighthouses become roofs and minarets and domes of some stately city of the clouds, and these melt in their turn, and the whole coast shrinks away to the merest line on the horizon immeasurably removed. Each of these changes, and the various aspects of their little world, are of inestimable value to the lonely children living always in that solitude. Nothing is too slight to be precious: the flashing of an oar-blade in the morning light; the twinkling of a gull's wings afar off, like a star in the yellow sunshine of the drowsy summer afternoon; the

8

water-spout waltzing away before the wild wind
that cleaves the sea from the advancing thunder-
cloud ; the distant showers that march about the
horizon, trailing their dusky fringes of falling rain
over sea and land ; every phase of the great thunder-storms that make glorious the weeks of July
and August, from the first floating film of cloud
that rises in the sky till the scattered fragments
of the storm stream eastward to form a background
for the rainbow, — all these things are of the
utmost importance to dwellers at the Isles of
Shoals.   There is something especially delightful
in the perfumes which stream across the sea after
showers, like a heavenly greeting from the land :
scents of hay and of clover, spice of pine woods,
balm of flowers come floating over the cool waves
on the wings of the west wind, and touch one like
a breath from Paradise.   Few sounds from the
shore reach the islands ; the booming of guns is
audible, and sometimes, when the wind is west, the
air is pierced with distant car-whistles, so very remote, however, that they are hardly to be recognized except by a practised ear.

There is a superstition among the islanders that
Philip Babb, or some evil-minded descendant of his,
still haunts Appledore ; and no consideration would

induce the more timid to walk alone after dark over a certain shingly beach on that island, at the top of a cove bearing Babb's name, — for there the uneasy spirit is oftenest seen. He is supposed to have been so desperately wicked when alive that there is no rest for him in his grave. His dress is a coarse, striped butcher's frock, with a leather belt, to which is attached a sheath containing a ghostly knife, sharp and glittering, which it is his delight to brandish in the face of terrified humanity. One of the Shoalers is perfectly certain that he and Babb have met, and he shudders with real horror, recalling the meeting. This is his story. It was after sunset (of course), and he was coming round the corner of a work-shop, when he saw a wild and dreadful figure advancing toward him; his first thought was that some one wished to make him the victim of a practical joke, and he called out something to the effect that he " was n't afraid "; but the thing came near with ghastly face and hollow eyes, and, assuming a fiendish expression, took out the knife from its belt and flourished it in the face of the Shoaler, who fled to the house and entered breathless, calling for the person who he supposed had tried to frighten him. That person was quietly eating his supper; and when the poor fellow saw him he was so much agitated that he nearly fainted, and his belief in Babb was fixed more firmly than ever. One spring night some one was sitting on the broad piazza at sunset; it was calm and mild; the sea murmured a little; birds twittered softly; there was hardly a waft of wind in the still atmosphere. Glancing toward Babb's Cove, he saw a figure slowly crossing the shingle to the path which led to the house. After watching it a moment he called to it, but there was no reply; again he called, still no answer; but the dark figure came slowly on; and then he reflected that he had heard no step on the loose shingle that was wont to give back every footfall, and, somewhat puzzled, he slowly descended the steps of the piazza and went to meet it. It was not so dark but that he could see the face and recognize the butcher's frock and leather belt of Babb, but he was not prepared for the devilish expression of malice in that hollow face, and, spite of his prosaic turn of mind, he was chilled to the marrow at the sight. The white stripes in the frock gleamed like phosphorescent light, so did the awful eyes. Again he called aloud, "Who are you? What do you want?" and still advanced, when suddenly the shape grew indistinct, first thick and cloudy, then thin, dissolving quite away, and, much amazed, he turned and went back to the house, perplexed and thoroughly dissatisfied. These tales I tell as they were told to me. I never saw Babb, nor ever could, I think. The whole Babb family are buried in the valley of Appledore where the houses stand, and till this year a bowling-alley stood upon the spot, and all the balls rolled over the bones of all the Babbs; that may have been one reason why the head of the family was so restless; since the last equinoctial gale blew the building down, perhaps he may rest more peacefully. Babb's is, I believe, the only real ghost that haunts the islands; though in the loft at the parsonage on Star (a mere creep-hole under the eaves, unattainable by any steps or ladder) there is, in windy weather, the most extraordinary combination of sounds, as if two bluff old fellows were swearing at each other, gruffly, harshly, continually, with a perseverance worthy of a better cause. Really, it is a most disagreeable racket! A lean, brown, hollow-eyed old woman from Star used to tell how her daughter-in-law died, in a way that took the color out of childish cheeks to hear; for the dying woman thought the ghosts were scratching for her outside, against the house. "'Ma'y Hahner'" (Mary Hannah), "she said to me, a whisperin', says she, 'Who's that scratching, tearing the house down underneath the window?' 'No, it ain't nothin',' says I ; 'Ma'y Hahner, there ain't nobody a tearin' the house down underneath the winder.' 'Yes, yes, there is,' says she, 'there is ! I hear 'em scratching, scratching, tearing the house down underneath the winder !' And then I know'd Ma'y Hahner was goin' to die, and so she did afore mornin'."

There is a superstition here and along the coast to this effect. A man gathering drift-wood or whatever it may be, sees a spade stuck in the ground as if inviting him to dig. He is n't quite ready, goes and empties his basket first, then comes back to investigate, and lo ! there 's nothing there, and he is tormented the rest of his life with the thought that probably untold wealth lay beneath that spade, which he might have possessed had he only been wise enough to seize the treasure when it offered itself. A certain man named William Mace, living at Star, long, long ago, swore that he had had this experience ; and there 's a dim tradition that another person, seeing the spade, passed by about his business, but hastening back, arrived just in time to see the last of the sinking tool, and to perceive also a golden flat-iron disappearing into the earth. This he seized, but no human power could extricate it from the ground, and he was forced to let go his hold and see it sink out of his longing ken.

Some young people, camping on the south side of Appledore, one summer, among the ancient graves, dug up a skeleton ; the bones crumbled to dust, but the skull remained intact, and I kept it for a long time. The Shoalers shook their heads. " Hog Island would have no ' luck' while that skull remained above ground." It had lain so long in the earth that it was no more repulsive than a bit of stone, yet a nameless dread invested it. At last I took it in my hands and pored over it till the shudder passed away forever, and then I was never weary of studying it. Sitting by the drift-wood blaze late into the still autumn nights alone at my desk, it kept me company, — a vase of brilliant flowers on one side, the skull on the other, and the shaded lamp between, equally lighting both. A curious head it was, thick as an Ethiop's, with no space above the eyes, high above the ears, and heavy behind them. But O, those hollows where the eyes once looked out, beholding the same sea and sky we see to-day ! Those great, melancholy, empty hollows, — what sort of creature gazed from them ? Cunning and malice, anger and hate, may have burned within them in sullen flame ; who shall say if any beauty ever illumined them ? If hate smouldered here, did love ever look out and transfigure the poor, dull face? did any spark from the far heaven ever brighten it? any touch of lofty thought or aspiration turn the clay to fire? And when, so many years ago, this being glided away from behind these awful windows and left them empty for ever and ever, did he find what in his life here he could not have possessed, with this head, which he did not make, and therefore was not responsible for? Many and many a question I put silently to the silent casket which had held a human soul; there was no sound to answer me save only the great, gentle whisper of the sea without the windows, and now and then a sigh from the autumn wind. There came to me a sense of the pathos of the infinite patience of humanity, waiting so helplessly and blindly for the unravelling of the riddle that has troubled every thoughtful soul since the beginning of time. Little roots of plants were clasped about the temples. Behind the right ear were three indentations, as if made by some sharp instrument, suggesting foul play. An Indian tomahawk might have made those marks, or a pirate's cutlass: who can say? What matter is it now? I kept the relic for months, till it crumbled so fast when I daily dusted it that I feared it would disappear entirely; so I carried it quietly back and laid it in the grave from which it had been taken, wondering, as I drew the shallow earth over it, who had stood round about when it was buried for the first time, centuries ago ; what manner of people, and were they afraid or sorry. But there was no voice to answer me.

I have before me a weird, romantic legend of these islands, in a time-stained, battered newspaper of forty years ago. I regret that it is too long to be given entire, for the unknown writer tells his story well. He came to the Shoals for the benefit of his failing health, and remained there late into the autumn of 1826, " in the family of a worthy fisherman." He dilates upon the pleasure he found in the loneliness of the place, " the vast solitude of the sea; no one who has not known it can imbibe the faintest idea of it." " From the hour I learned the truth," he says, " that all which lives must die, the thought of dissolution has haunted me ; — the falling of a leaf, a gray hair, or a faded cheek, has power to chill me. But here in the recesses of these eternal rocks, with only a cloudless sky above and an ocean before me, for the first time in my life have I shaken off the fear of death and believed myself immortal."

He tells his strange story in this way : " It was one of those awfully still mornings which cloud-

8 *   L

gazers will remember as characterizing the autumn
months.   There was not a single vapor-wreath to
dim the intense blue of the sky, or a breath to
ruffle the almost motionless repose of the great
deep ; even the sunlight fell seemingly with stiller
brightness on the surface of it."   He stood on a
low, long point fronting the east, with the cliffs
behind him, gazing out upon the calm, when suddenly he became aware of a figure standing near
him.   It was a woman wrapped closely in a dark
sea-cloak, with a profusion of light hair flowing
loosely over her shoulders.   Fair as a lily and as
still, she stood with her eyes fixed on the far distance, without a motion, without a sound.   "Thinking her one of the inhabitants of a neighboring
island who was watching for the return of a fish-
ing-boat, or perhaps a lover, I did not immediately
address her ; but seeing no appearance of any vessel, at length accosted her with, 'Well, my
pretty maiden, do you see anything of him?'   She
turned instantly, and fixing on me the largest and
most melancholy blue eyes I ever beheld, said
quietly, 'He *will* come again.'"   Then she disappeared round a jutting rock and left him marvelling, and though he had come to the island (which
was evidently Appledore) for a forenoon's stroll,
he was desirous to get back again to Star and his

own quarters after this interruption. Fairly at
home again, he was inclined to look upon his ad-
venture as a dream, a mere delusion arising from
his illness, but concluded to seek in his surround-
ings something to substantiate, or remove the idea.
Finding nothing, — no woman on the island resem-
bling the one he had met, — and " hearing of no
circumstance which might corroborate the unac-
countable impression," he resolved to go again to
the same spot.   This time it blew half a gale ; the
fishermen in vain endeavored to dissuade him.   He
was so intensely anxious to be assured of the
truth or fiction of the impression of the day before, that he could not refrain, and launched his
boat, " which sprang strongly upon the whitened
waters," and, unfurling his one sail, he rounded a
point and was soon safely sheltered in a small cove
on the leeward side of the island, probably Babb's
Cove.

Then he leaped the chasms and made his way to
the scene of his bewilderment.   The sea was rolling over the low point ; the spot where he had
stood the day before, " was a chaos of tumult, yet
even then I could have sworn that I heard with
the same deep distinctness, the quiet words of the
maiden, 'He *will* come again,' and then a low,
remotely-ringing laughter.   All the latent super-

stition of my nature rose up over me, overwhelming as the waves upon the rocks." After that, day after day, when the weather would permit, he visited the desolate place, to find the golden-haired ghost, and often she stood beside him, "silent as when I first saw her, except to say, as then, 'He *will* come again,' and these words came upon the mind rather than upon the ear. I was conscious of them rather then heard them, — it was all like a dream, a mysterious intuition. I observed that the shells never crashed beneath her footsteps, nor did her garments rustle. In the bright, awful calm of noon and in the rush of the storm there was the same heavy stillness over her. When the winds were so furious that I could scarcely stand in their sweep, the light hair lay upon the forehead of the maiden without lifting a fibre. Her great blue eyeballs never moved in their sockets, and always shone with the same fixed, unearthly gleam. The motion of her person was imperceptible; I knew that she was here, and that she was gone."

So sweet a ghost was hardly a salutary influence in the life of our invalid. She "held him with her glittering eye" till he grew quite beside himself. This is so good a description I cannot choose but quote it: "The last time I stood with her, was

VIEW FROM THE SOUTHEASTERN POINT OF APPLEDORE.

The Appledore house and the swimming pool. A corner of the author's cottage and garden is at left. The hotel was owned and operated by the author's family. This book was intended as a guide for the summer visitors to the islands.

The author's cottage on Appledore. The fence surrounds her famous flower garden.

just at the evening of a tranquil day. It was a lovely sunset. A few gold-edged clouds crowned the hills of the distant continent, and the sun had gone down behind them. The ocean lay blushing beneath the blushes of the sky, and even the ancient rocks seemed smiling in the glance of the departing day. Peace, deep peace was the pervading power. The waters, lapsing among the caverns, spoke of it, and it was visible in the silent motion of the small boats, which, loosening their white sails in the cove of Star Island, passed slowly out, one by one, to the night-fishing." In the glow of sunset he fancied the ghost grew rosy and human. In the mellow light her cold eyes seemed to soften. But he became suddenly so overpowered with terror that " kneeling in shuddering fearfulness, he swore never more to look upon that spot, and never did again."

Going back to Star he met his old fisherman, who without noticing his agitation, told him quietly that he knew where he had been and what he had seen ; that he himself had seen her, and proceeded to furnish him with the following facts. At the time of the first settlement, the islands were infested by pirates, — the bold Captain Teach, called Blackbeard, being one of the most notorious. One of Teach's comrades, a Captain Scot, brought this lovely lady hither. They buried immense treasure on the islands ; that of Scot was buried on an island apart from the rest. Before they departed on a voyage, "to plunder, slash, and slay," (in which, by the way, they were involved in one awful doom by the blowing up of a powder magazine), the maiden was carried to the island where her pirate lover's treasure was hidden, and made to swear with horrible rites that until his return, if it were not till the day of judgment, she would guard it from the search of all mortals. So there she paces still, according to our story-teller. Would I had met this lily-fair ghost ! Is it she, I wonder, who laments like a Banshee before the tempests, wailing through the gorges at Appledore, " He will *not* come again " ? Perhaps it was she who frightened a merry party of people at Duck Island, whither they had betaken themselves for a day's pleasure a few summers ago. In the centre of the low island stood a deserted shanty which some strange fishermen had built there several years before, and left empty, tenanted only by the mournful winds. It was blown down the September following. It was a rude hut with two rough rooms and one square window, or rather opening for a window, for sash or glass there was none. One of our party proposed going to look after the

boats, as the breeze freshened and blew directly
upon the cove where we had landed. We were
gathered on the eastern end of the island when he
returned, and, kneeling on the withered grass where
we were grouped, he said suddenly, " Do you know
what I have seen ? Coming back from the boats,
I faced the fish-house, and as I neared it I saw
some one watching me from the window. Of
course I thought it was one of you, but when I
was near enough to have recognized it, I perceived
it to be the strange countenance of a woman, wan
as death ; a face young, yet with a look in it of
infinite age. Old ! it was older than the Sphinx
in the desert ! It looked as if it had been watching and waiting for me since the beginning of
time. I walked straight into the hut. There
was n't a vestige of a human being there ; it was
absolutely empty. " All the warmth and brightness of the summer day could hardly prevent a
chill from creeping into our veins as we listened to
this calmly delivered statement, and we actually
sent a boat back to Appledore for a large yacht to
take us home, for the wind rose fast and " gurly
grew the sea," and we half expected the wan
woman would come and carry our companion off
bodily before our eyes.

Since writing these imperfect sketches of the

Shoals it has become an historical fact for the records of the State of New Hampshire that the town of Gosport has disappeared, is obliterated from the face of the earth, nearly all the inhabitants having been bought out, that the place might be converted into a summer resort. Upon Appledore a large house of entertainment has been extending its capabilities for many years, and the future of the Shoals as a famous watering-place may be considered certain.

The slight sprinkling of inhabitants yet remaining on Smutty-nose and elsewhere, who seem inclined to make of the place a permanent home, are principally Swedes and Norwegians; and a fine, self-respecting race they are, so thrifty, cleanly, well-mannered, and generally excellent that one can hardly say enough in their praise. It is to be hoped that a little rill from the tide of emigration which yearly sets from those countries toward America may finally people the unoccupied portions of the Shoals with a colony that will be a credit to New England.

INDEX